cookie
magic

Kate Shirazi

Photography by Charlotte Barton

PAVILION

First published in the United Kingdom in 2009 by
Pavilion Books
10 Southcombe Street
London W14 0RA

An imprint of Anova Books Company Ltd

Commissioning editor: Emily Preece-Morrison
Designer: Anna Pow
Cover design: Georgina Hewitt
Home economist: Kate Shirazi
Photography and styling: Charlotte Barton
Case illustration: Lotte Oldfield
Copy editor: Kathy Steer
Proofreader: Alyson Silverwood
Indexer: Patricia Hymans

ISBN 978-1-862058-47-7

A CIP catalogue record for this book is available from the British Library.

10 9 8 7 6 5 4

Reproduction by Dot Gradations Ltd, United Kingdom
Printed and bound by Times Offset Malaysia Sdn Bhd

www.anovabooks.com

Contents

Introduction

When I was growing up there were three words, which I heard every single day until I was about 12: 'juice and biscuits'. Blooming marvellous. At elevenses and mid afternoon – often on our return from school – this was the standard snack. Juice actually meant weak squash (orange or lemon – none of your fancy schmancy forest-fruit-with-a-hint-of-hibiscus) and two biscuits. *Never* more than two: two was the standard portion size, and indeed I have held on to the two biscuit rule with my son too. It is thoroughly ingrained and cannot be changed. The biscuits were, more often than not, plain. Digestives, Rich Tea or very occasionally Garibaldi (squashed fly biscuits). Chocolate biscuits were for parties or very special occasions, as was anything containing a cream filling. Those biscuits were the stuff of dreams, and long discussions about the merits of a Lemon Puff over a Jammy Dodger ensued. I always favoured a layered biscuit (wafer, any sort of cream sandwich or tea cake), which could be dissected while it was eaten.

I remember when chocolate chip cookies started appearing in my mother's shopping. Oh my word, the excitement! They looked American (excellent), weren't digestives or Rich Tea (also excellent) and contained chocolate (whimper). However, I had one complaint about these biscuits, which holds to this day. They are very small. Remember the two biscuit rule? Well, it stood even with small biscuits. Hmmm.

Well, 'juice and biscuits' may have disappeared from my regular vocabulary, but 'biscuit' certainly hasn't. 'No, you've already had two' is a common phrase, as is 'But MUM, they weren't very big.' The squash seems to have disappeared altogether, but in my world there's nothing

that goes better with a cup of tea than a biscuit. Coffee seems to have changed all the rules too. In the seventies, coffee mornings were big news, with plates of biscuits handed round (generally not very special ones either...). I never really understood the concept of the coffee morning, but then, I was seven, dragged along by Mum who had to attend for some reason or another. Anyway, in those days, coffee also meant biscuits. Nowadays, coffee has gone bonkers and is a meal itself. A skinny Lattechinomochafresco doesn't really shout, 'Oooh, I do need a biscuit. Do not even think about taking a sip without a biscuit on my saucer.' For starters, there isn't usually a saucer. Whereas a lovely cup of Earl Grey positively bellows, 'Where's the biscuit? Where's the biscuit?' See what I mean?

But why make a biscuit yourself when there are so many delicious varieties available on a supermarket shelf near you? I'll tell you why: they are easy and they are super-duper delicious, you know exactly what goes into them and they give you a very warm glow of self-satisfaction when you and your chosen ones eat them. You don't get that from a packet of Morning Coffee (possibly the worst biscuit in the world). Most of the dough-based recipes in the book are really handy in that you can make the dough, freeze it, and just pluck it out of the freezer, slice bits off the frozen log and bake straight away. Biscuits in 10 minutes, literally.

The ingredients in the book are pretty straightforward. Most of the stuff can be bought in the supermarket, but anything you can't get there can be found in a health food store. If you can't find decorative frivolities, there are lots of brilliant online shops, which will send you a parcel full of excitement (after you have paid them, of course). These places are also an Aladdin's cave for cookie cutters. Pop what you want into a search engine ('sugar craft suppliers' is a good start) and *voilà* – a cornucopia of delights.

The one bit of kit I think is absolutely critical, vital and without which your biscuit-making experience is going to be a lot less enjoyable is re-usable silicone linings. I cannot praise them highly enough and I really wouldn't even consider starting to make a biscuit without one on my baking sheet. They are washable and re-usable. I bought a roll of this magic stuff about three years ago and cut it to fit the size of my baking sheets. It's still in action. Sometimes a cursory wipe is even enough if I'm feeling particularly slovenly. *Nothing* sticks to it. Ever.

I am usually pretty laid back when it comes to ingredients and am not at all precious about whether a nut is flaked, baked or tied in a bow, but there are two exceptions. With these exceptions I am going to get jolly cross if I find out you have disobeyed my orders. Butter and eggs. If a recipe in this small and, quite frankly, informal tome asks for butter, for goodness' sake use it. I honestly don't give a monkey's if you use salted or unsalted. But you do need to know that unsalted butter makes nicer biscuits, and all the recipes here are really based on using unsalted butter. There are a few recipes where using salted butter isn't a good idea – Rich Tea and Custard Creams being the main ones – but I have made it clear when you do need to use unsalted. Margarine will make biscuits taste foul and the consistency will be wrong. Even that spreadable butter is no good – it's too soft – don't do it.

Now ... eggs. My mantra has now become 'are the eggs free range?' whenever we go out. I might get it tattooed somewhere ... perhaps not. Anyway, please, please, please buy and use free-range eggs. Eggs laid by caged hens are *not* acceptable. It's funny how people are

quite happy to veto veal (even the pink veal, which is fine, but that's another story), but will happily gorge themselves on eggs laid by caged hens. Veal crate/hen cage – tell me the difference, because I can't see it.

I keep hens and the hens I keep come to me from the Battery Hen Welfare Trust (www.bhwt.org.uk). These are hens that have been intercepted on their way to the slaughterhouse. These hens are bald when they come to me. They have never been outside, have never had room to flap their wings, have never felt the wind in their feathers, have never had a dust bath, perched, walked (let alone run), never tried to escape from their really large run, never destroyed a vegetable patch, chased a cat, stolen a loaf of bread or decimated a picnic. Please buy free-range eggs. Yes they are a bit more expensive, but I really, really think it's money well spent. The more people who buy them, the more we encourage food manufacturers and supermarkets to go free range, the more farmers will have the economic incentive to farm free-range hens. Thank you. Lecture over.

Now we need to have a full and frank discussion about how many biscuits each recipe makes. I'm getting all tense writing this, I'll have you know. Most recipe books have a little bit saying 'makes 24 biscuits' or something similar. This book will not. Each recipe will make one batch – a do-able, edible batch. You shouldn't have so few as to to make it not worthwhile and you shouldn't have too many so you are eating them for weeks. The problem with stating numbers is that I positively *want* you to use different sorts of cutters. How the devil do you work out how many biscuits would be made using a heart-shaped cutter, if someone decides to use a giant T-Rex cutter? If you roll the dough two more times than me, you'll have a thinner biscuit and you'll get more. Do you see my point? My small teaspoon is

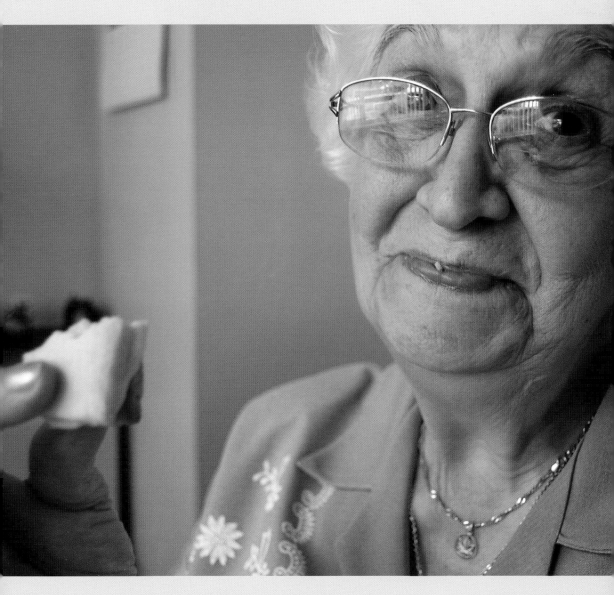

going to be different from your small teaspoon. Embrace the unknown, just make the biscuits and enjoy them – don't let yourself get hung up on the fact that a recipe says 'makes 24' and you've got 12 – or 45. And another thing in the same vein ... my oven is different to your oven. And your oven is different to your friend's oven. Take the cooking times with a pinch of salt. Look at the biscuits. Are they burnt? You've probably left them in the oven too long. Is there acrid smoke pouring out of the oven? I'd say you've definitely overdone it. You know your oven; believe in your ability to know when something is cooked. Remember, biscuits do crisp up after they come out of the oven, so it's the colour that is the best guide for 'doneness'.

The other little point is how long they keep for. Again, it depends on how you store them. Real biscuits go stale quicker than shop-bought ones. I reckon on a good four or five days in a biscuit tin with a tight lid. I bet they don't hang around for that long though....

I feel I should add a note for my friends from 'across the pond'. I realize that when I mention 'biscuits' you are visualizing something entirely different from what we Brits call 'biscuits'. So every time you see the word, substitute it for 'cookie' if you like. Though a subtle distinction, and there are recipes here for soft cookies as well as biscuits, I am British and so make tea in a pot with tea leaves, enjoy gardening and call a biscuit a biscuit. Sorry, but there we have it!

I hope you enjoy making these biscuits and cookies. Amaze yourself by the speed at which you can knock them up and relish the deliciousness. I'm not saying you'll never buy another packet of biscuits again, but I tell you, you'll think twice before reaching for the packet of Morning Coffee.

Everyday

Everyday biscuits mean those ones that routinely fill the biscuit tin and give you a comforting feeling when you think about what lies therein. It might be a Digestive (I implore you to try these), a Custard Cream or even a Rich Tea. These are biscuits that aren't hugely extravagant to make, are jolly easy and fit the bill when you want a little something for elevenses or mid afternoon.

You might recognize some of the biscuits – Digestives, Bourbons and Custard Creams are all old chums, but the trick is not to try and imitate a shop-bought version. What on earth would be the point? What you are after is a superior version of a Digestive or a biscuit that you recognize as a Bourbon, but somehow better. The one I am most proud of is the Rich Tea. A dullard if ever there was one, but though I say so myself, my version is a rather cheeky little number with all sorts of hidden talents.

Some of these biscuit recipes require making a dough, which needs to be refrigerated. Please don't miss this out as an extra 'fidaddle' (just made that word up, but I think it's a good 'un) that can be avoided. Well, you can if you want, but you'll be cursing and stropping as you try and roll out the dough. If time is of the essence, there are plenty of recipes that can go directly into the oven – some via the rolling pin and others via the spoon. I aim to please.

Basic butter biscuit

This, to me, is the holy grail of biscuits. It's a simple, foolproof recipe that makes delicious biscuits 'au naturelle', but the beauty of it is that it can be endlessly tampered with without many ill effects.

✳ Makes 1 batch

250 g/9 oz/generous 1 cup
  butter, softened
140 g/5 oz/scant 1 cup icing
  (confectioners') sugar, sifted
1 tsp vanilla extract
1 large free-range egg yolk
375 g/13 oz/2¾ cups plain
  (all-purpose) flour, plus extra
  for dusting

Beat the butter and sugar together in a large bowl until very pale and fluffy. Add the vanilla and egg yolk and mix well. Sift in the flour and mix until it forms a firm dough. You may need to get your hands in here and work it into a smooth ball. Wrap the dough in cling film and plonk it in the refrigerator for an hour. You can freeze it at this stage very happily if you wish.

Preheat the oven to 190°C/375°F/Gas Mark 5 and line 2 baking sheets with a silicone liner.

Roll out the dough on a lightly floured surface until it is about 3 mm/⅛ inch thick, then cut out the shapes you require and place on your lined baking sheets. Bake for 10–12 minutes or until the biscuits are pale golden. Transfer the biscuits to a wire rack where they will harden as they cool. Yum.

Basic shortbread

Another humdinger, this shortbread is a treat by itself, but is also the basis for endless variations on a theme. It is very easy to make and utterly delicious. Perfectomondo.

✳ Makes 1 batch

250 g/9 oz/generous 1 cup butter, softened, plus extra for greasing (if needed)
50 g/2 oz/¼ cup caster (superfine) sugar
250 g/9 oz/1¾ cups plain (all-purpose) flour
125 g/4½ oz/1 cup cornflour (cornstarch)

Preheat the oven to 170°C/325°F/Gas Mark 3.

Cream the butter and sugar together in a large bowl until pale and fluffy. Sift the flour and cornflour on to the butter mixture and mix until you have a lovely smooth dough. At this stage you can either press it into a square tin, which you have lightly greased, and bake straight away or form it into a fat sausage and wrap it in cling film. Make the sausage as fat as you want the biscuits to be round and chill the dough in the refrigerator for at least an hour.

Unwrap the dough and slice into rounds about 1.5 cm/ ⅝ inch thick. Place the rounds on a silicone-lined baking tray and bake for about 30–40 minutes until pale and golden. Transfer the shortbread to a wire tray to cool.

If you are using a tin, cut the shortbread in the tin while it is still warm and leave to cool in the tin.

Rich Tea

I think of Rich Tea biscuits as the ultimate in functional everyday biscuits – slightly frugal and, if I'm honest, not that enjoyable, but something to dunk into a cup of tea. It's a puritanical biscuit – it will not lead you into wickedness. I think this version might possibly make you consider toying with wickedness, if not actually going the whole hog. They are plain, but like all those secretaries in *James Bond* films, when they whip off their glasses, 'why – Miss Jones, you are beautiful...' Just one word of warning: they really, really do need to be made with unsalted butter. Sorry.

✳ Makes 1 batch

225 g/8 oz/1⅔ cups plain
  (all-purpose) flour, plus extra
  for dusting
1 tbsp baking powder (yes, really)
75 g/3 oz/scant ½ cup caster
  (superfine) sugar
¼ tsp salt
175 g/6 oz/¾ cup unsalted butter,
  cubed
A little milk

Preheat the oven to 190°C/375°F/Gas Mark 5 and line 2 baking sheets with silicone liners.

Place all the dry ingredients in a large bowl, then add the butter and rub it in with your fingertips until you have a consistency of fine breadcrumbs. Add enough milk, a dessertspoon at a time, until you have a firm dough (generally, I use 2–3 spoons). You don't need to chill the dough, but it keeps well in the refrigerator for about 3 days if you want to make it in advance.

Roll out the dough on a lightly floured surface as thin as you can, about 2 mm/¹⁄₁₆ inch would be good if possible. Cut out circle shapes and place them on your lined baking sheets. Prod them all over with a fork and bake for 8–10 minutes until golden. Transfer the biscuits to a wire rack to cool.

Digestives

I did wonder whether it was a bit risky putting in a recipe for the digestive, which has to be one of the most recognizable and un-mucked-about biscuits in the UK. If you are reading this outside the UK, you'll have to believe me – they are an institution. All I'll say is, no, they are not identical to those ones in the red packet, but they do contain the 'essence of digestive'. By jiminy they are good: easy, economical and comforting. All the things a digestive should be.

✳ Makes 1 batch

100 g/4 oz/⅔ cup wholemeal (whole-wheat) flour
40 g/1½ oz/¼ cup plain white (all-purpose) flour, plus extra for dusting
½ tsp baking powder
1 tbsp oats
120 g/4½ oz/9 tbsp butter, softened
100 g/4 oz/½ cup soft light brown sugar
4 tbsp milk

Preheat the oven to 190°C/375°F/Gas Mark 5 and line 2 baking sheets with silicone liners.

Mix the flours, baking powder and oats together in a large bowl. In another bowl, cream the butter and sugar together and add the flour mix to this. Stir in the milk, a little at a time, until you have a thick dough.

Knead the dough on a floured surface until it's lovely and smooth (albeit speckled slightly with the oats), then roll out to about 3 mm/⅛ inch thick and cut into rounds. Plonk them on your lined baking sheets, prick all over with a fork and bake for about 15 minutes until golden.

Transfer the biscuits to a wire rack to cool, then store them in an airtight tin. Put the kettle on...

Ginger biscuits

You can't have a biscuit book without ginger biscuits. It would be wrong. These are the unsophisticated, gorgeously moreish ones that positively reek of ground ginger and which are very popular with both children and adults. A biscuit with no drawbacks as far as I am concerned.

✳ Makes 1 batch

150 g/5 oz/generous 1 cup
   self-raising (self-rising) flour
½ tsp bicarbonate of soda
   (baking soda)
2 tsp ground ginger
1 tsp ground cinnamon
2 tsp caster (superfine) sugar
50 g/2 oz/4 tbsp butter
2 tbsp golden (corn) syrup

Preheat the oven to 190°C/375°F/Gas Mark 5 and line 2 baking sheets with silicone liners.

Sift together all the dry ingredients in a large bowl. Heat the butter and golden syrup gently in a pan and when the butter has melted, pour it over the dry ingredients. Mix well until you have a soft dough. If it's a bit sticky, sprinkle a little more flour on to it until you get a consistency you can comfortably handle.

Using your hands, form small balls of the mixture, flatten them slightly and place them on your lined baking sheets, allowing a little space between them as they spread. Bake for about 15 minutes until golden and gorgeous-looking.

Let the biscuits cool and harden on the baking sheets for a bit before lifting them on to wire racks to cool completely.

Anzac biscuits

An old colleague of mine, Ros, introduced me to Anzac biscuits. I was completely smitten with them – chewy, oaty, coconutty and just plain old yummy. Luckily for me she gave me the recipe. I understand that they were originally made by the women of the Australian and New Zealand Army Corps (ANZAC) for the men during World War 1. Another little interesting fact: they are never to be known as 'cookies', but must always be referred to as 'biscuits'. It's the law. Look online if you don't believe me!

❋ Makes 1 batch

100 g/4 oz/1⅓ cups rolled oats
150 g/5 oz/generous 1 cup plain (all-purpose) flour
100 g/4 oz/½ cup soft light brown sugar
50 g/2 oz/scant ½ cup desiccated (dry unsweetened) coconut
115 g/4 oz/8 tbsp butter
2 tbsp golden (corn) syrup
1 tbsp hot water
½ tsp bicarbonate of soda (baking soda)

Preheat the oven to 190°C/375°F/Gas Mark 5 and line 2 baking sheets with silicone liners.

Mix the oats, flour, sugar and coconut together in a large bowl. Heat the butter and golden syrup gently in a pan until the butter has melted.

In another bowl, mix the hot water and bicarbonate of soda together and add the mixture to the pan of butter and golden syrup. Watch out for froth-central, then tip the whole lot on top of the oat mixture and stir away. Plop dessertspoonfuls of the mixture on to your lined baking sheets, allowing a little space between them as they spread, and flatten slightly. Bake for about 10 minutes until golden.

Let the biscuits cool and set on the baking sheets for a few minutes before lifting them onto wire racks to cool completely.

Custard creams

I *really* love Custard Creams. So it was always going to be a bit of a struggle to find a recipe that did them justice. I have experimented, trialled, jiggled and wiggled, and I have to say that this one is good. It is an adaptation of a recipe by she-who-must-be-obeyed, Nigella Lawson.

✳ Makes 1 batch

175 g/6 oz/1 ¼ cups plain (all-purpose) flour, plus extra for dusting
3 tbsp custard powder (not the sachets you add hot water to – proper custard powder)
1 tsp baking powder
60 g/2 ½ oz/4 ½ tbsp unsalted butter
60 g/2 ½ oz/4 ½ tbsp white vegetable fat
3 tbsp icing (confectioners') sugar
1 large free-range egg
1 tbsp milk

Filling:
50 g/2 oz/4 tbsp unsalted butter, softened
1 tbsp custard powder
100 g/4 oz/1 cup icing (confectioners') sugar, sifted
Few drops of hot water (optional)

✳ Pictured on the far right of the image on p.13.

Preheat the oven to 190°C/350°F/Gas Mark 5 and line 2 baking sheets with silicone liners.

Pop the flour, custard powder and baking powder into a large bowl. Cut the butter and white fat into little pieces and rub them into the dry ingredients until you have the consistency of sand. Add the sugar and mix until it is well combined.

In another bowl, beat the eggs lightly with the milk and pour on to the flour mixture, then mix it well (go on, get yer hands in there) and form it into a ball. Wrap the dough in cling film and leave to chill in the refrigerator for at least 30 minutes. You can freeze it at this stage too – handy.

Roll out the dough on a lightly floured surface until it is about 3 mm/⅛ inch thick. Cut the sheet of dough into long strips about 3 cm/1 ¼ inches wide and then cut the strips into 4 cm/1 ½ inch lengths. Lay the little biscuits on your lined baking sheets and bake for about 15 minutes.

Transfer the biscuits to a wire rack to cool while you make the filling. Cream the butter, custard powder and sugar together in a large bowl until light and fluffy. If the mixture seems a little stiff, add a few drops of hot water and beat it in until it is the consistency you are after. Sandwich 2 biscuits together with the creamy, custardy filling and enjoy.

Lemon biscuits (mark one)

This is another easy peasy classic biscuit, which is just lemony enough to brighten up a dull day.

✳ Makes 1 batch

1 batch Basic Butter Biscuit dough (see p.14), but omit the vanilla extract
Finely grated zest and juice of 1 large unwaxed lemon
Plain (all-purpose) flour, for dusting
50 g/2 oz/½ cup icing (confectioners') sugar, sifted

Make up the biscuit dough according to the instructions on page 14 and add the lemon zest. Knead it in well until it is evenly distributed. Cover the dough and leave to chill in the refrigerator for about an hour.

Preheat the oven to 190°C/375°F/Gas Mark 5 and line a baking sheet with a silicone liner.

Roll the dough out on a lightly floured surface to a thickness of about 3 mm/⅛ inch and cut out circle shapes. They don't have to be circles, they can be elephant shapes if you want, but I always make circular lemon biscuits. I don't know why. I just do. Place them on your lined baking sheet and bake for 10–12 minutes or until the biscuits are pale golden.

Transfer to a wire rack to cool. Once they are cold, make up a simple and quite runny lemon icing with the sugar and lemon juice. Since lemons don't come with a message stating how much juice they contain, may I suggest that you thin the icing with a few drops of hot water or thicken it with a smidgen more icing sugar until it is the consistency of single cream. Drizzle the icing randomly over the biscuits and leave to dry and harden before putting in an airtight tin (or in your mouth).

Lemon biscuits (mark two)

I think lemon and almond go particularly well together. These are really easy to make and as an added extra, don't even need rolling out. They are also very versatile. If you don't want lemony ones (how odd), omit the zest and add whatever jam takes your fancy.

✳ Makes 1 batch

110 g/4 oz/½ cup caster (superfine) sugar
220 g/7½ oz/scant 1 cup butter, softened
60 g/2½ oz/⅔ cup icing (confectioners') sugar
1 large free-range egg yolk
150 g/5 oz/1⅔ cups ground almonds
1 tsp almond extract
Finely grated zest and juice of 1 large unwaxed lemon
300 g/10 oz/1½ cups plain (all-purpose) flour
1 tsp baking powder
1 x small jar of lemon curd (you'll need about 120 g/4½ oz or so)

Preheat the oven to 190°C/375°F/Gas Mark 5 and line 2 baking sheets with silicone liners.

Beat the caster sugar and butter together in a large bowl until very pale and fluffy. Beat in the icing sugar, egg yolk, ground almonds, almond extract, zest and 2 teaspoons of the lemon juice. Give it a good thrashing. Sift in the flour and baking powder and stir until everything is combined.

Form a blob of the mixture into a ball just a bit smaller than a golf ball and place on your lined baking sheets. Keep going, leaving a space between all your golf balls. With your thumb, squish down to form a little well in the now flattened ball and fill with a little dollop of lemon curd (not too much or it will overflow and burn). Bake for about 10–12 minutes until the biscuits are golden and gorgeous.

Transfer to a wire rack to cool.

WARNING: don't be greedy and eat them while warm – the lemon curd will still be molten hot.

Lemon puffs

These biscuits in their traditional, shop-bought form seem to be in the league of 'love them or loathe them'. This version is less challenging and an absolute cinch to make. I would say though, that unlike most of the biscuits in this book, they do need eating on the day you make them.

Preheat the oven to 200°C/400°F/Gas Mark 6 and line 2 baking sheets with silicone liners.

Place the pastry on a lightly floured surface and give it a couple of extra rolls in both directions – you just want to thin it out a tiny bit more. Cut the pastry into strips about 3 cm/1⅛ inches wide and then cut those strips into 3 cm/1⅛ inch squares. Prod them several times with a fork and place them on your lined baking sheets.

In a little bowl, break up the egg white with a fork, then add the caster sugar and lemon juice and whisk with a fork just enough to amalgamate it. You don't want to add air to the egg white. Using a pastry brush, carefully brush a little of the mixture over the top of each pastry square. Try not to spill too much mixture over the edge of the pastry as it will burn on the tray. Sprinkle each square with a little more caster sugar and bake for about 10 minutes until they are puffy and golden. Keep an eye on them because once burnt they are horrid. Transfer the biscuits to a wire rack to cool.

To make the filling, cream the butter and icing sugar together in a large bowl until light and fluffy, then beat in the lemon zest. If the mixture is a bit thick, add the lemon juice slowly until you have a spreadable consistency. Once the pastry squares are cool, sandwich 2 together with the lemon butter cream.

✳ Makes 1 batch

375 g/13 oz packet ready-rolled
    puff pastry
Plain (all-purpose) flour,
    for dusting
1 large free-range egg white
2 tsp caster (superfine) sugar,
    plus extra for sprinkling
Juice of ½ lemon

Filling:
50 g/2 oz/4 tbsp butter, softened
100 g/4 oz/½ cup icing
    (confectioners') sugar, sifted
Grated zest of 1 unwaxed lemon
Juice of ½ lemon (optional)

Macaroons Vegas style

Now, there seem to be as many ways to make these little beauties as there are days in the week. I've plumped for the one which uses minimum ingredients and has maximum deliciousness. I do have a tendency to slither towards my pots of colours and tint all sorts of food inappropriately. I'm sorry, I can't help it. There is an argument for having coloured coconut macaroons in the children's section of the book, but as the colour is entirely optional, it's here instead. If you do use colours, use a tiny, tiny drop of liquid food colouring, or a dab of food colouring paste, which you can buy in sugar craft shops. Go for colour, I say.

✳ Makes 1 batch

175 g/6 oz/1¼ cups desiccated
    (dry unsweetened) coconut
4 large free-range egg whites
110 g/4 oz/½ cup caster
    (superfine) sugar
Tiny pinch of salt
Food colouring (optional)

Preheat the oven to 190°C/375°F/Gas Mark 5 and line 2 baking sheets with silicone liners.

Place everything except the food colouring (if using) in a large heatproof bowl and give it a good stir, then place the bowl over a pan of barely simmering water. Do not let the base of the bowl touch the water. Stir constantly (can be quite gentle – nothing too arduous) for 5–6 minutes until the mixture suddenly changes consistency and goes really thick and gooey – you'll know when you get there, believe me.

If you are going for the natural look, place spoonfuls of the mixture (as big as you want the macaroons to be as they do not spread very much) on to your lined baking sheets, then flatten them slightly and pop them in the oven. If you want coloured ones, divide the mixture into as many bowls as you want colours and tint away, before spooning blobs on to your baking sheets. Bake for about 15 minutes until golden, then leave to cool on a wire rack.

Nutty noodles

When I was a child I remember doing a lot of baking and once made some peanut butter biscuits. I was very excited by the recipe and thought they sounded delicious. They were possibly the most revolting thing ever to have been created in our kitchen and scarred me psychologically, they were so bad. It was with some trepidation I started experimenting again with peanut butter biscuits. I am so glad I did. Not only have my scars healed without the expense of a private counsellor, but I am now officially keen on peanut butter biscuits.

✳ Makes 1 batch

110 g/4 oz/8 tbsp butter,
   softened
110 g/4 oz/8 tbsp soft light
   brown sugar
50 g/2 oz crunchy peanut butter
1 large free-range egg
275 g/10 oz/2 cups plain
   (all-purpose) flour
100 g/4 oz/⅔ cup honey-roasted
   peanuts, roughly chopped

Preheat the oven to 190°C/375°F/ Gas Mark 5 and line 2 baking sheets with silicone liners.

Cream the butter and sugar together in a large bowl until pale and fluffy, then beat in the peanut butter and egg. Stir in the flour and add the chopped peanuts.

Grab a small ball of the dough (as big as you want your biscuits), roll it into a ball and flatten it with your fingers until it is about 5 mm/¼ inch thick then place on your lined sheet. Keep going until you have used up all the dough. Bake for 10-15 minutes until golden then leave the biscuits to cool on a wire rack.

Bourbons

These biscuits are yet another classic. All I'd ask is that you use a really good quality cocoa powder. It makes all the difference. This dough is a dream to handle and the resulting biscuits are far more chocolatey than the shop-bought ones. Lovely.

✳ Makes 1 batch

50 g/2 oz/4 tbsp butter, softened
50 g/2 oz/¼ cup caster (superfine) sugar
1 tbsp golden (corn) syrup
110 g/4 oz/¾ cup plain (all-purpose) flour, plus extra for dusting
½ tsp bicarbonate of soda (baking soda)
15 g/½ oz cocoa powder

Filling:
50 g/2 oz/4 tbsp butter, softened
100 g/4 oz/1 cup icing (confectioners') sugar, sifted
2 tsp cocoa powder
Few drops of hot water (optional)

Preheat the oven to 190°C/375°F/Gas Mark 5 and line 2 baking sheets with silicone liners.

Cream the butter and sugar together in a large bowl until it is pale and fluffy, then beat in the golden syrup. Sift in the flour, bicarbonate of soda and cocoa, and mix until you have a stiff dough.

Knead the dough well, then roll the dough out on a floured surface to a depth of about 4 mm/¼ inch. Cut the dough into long strips about 2.5 cm/1 inch wide, then cut these strips into 5 cm/2 inch lengths. Transfer them to your lined baking trays and prod them several times with a fork. Bake for about 15 minutes until darkened slightly and smelling all chocolatey. What you want to watch out for is slight scorching around the edges. Whip them out of the oven if you see this.

Transfer the biscuits to a wire rack to cool while you make the filling. Cream the butter, icing sugar and cocoa together in a large bowl, adding a few drops of hot water if you need to, until you have a good, spreadable consistency.

When the biscuits are cold, sandwich 2 biscuits together and leave for at least an hour before eating so that the filling can firm up.

Oo-oo biscuits

Right, they are called oo-oo biscuits because people say 'oo' when they see them and then 'ooooooo' when they taste them. And calling them cinnamon-nut-crispy-biscuits seemed too dull. They are in the everyday section because, although impressive-looking, they are very easy.

✳ Makes 1 batch

110 g/4 oz/½ cup caster (superfine) sugar
275 g/10 oz/2 cups plain (all-purpose) flour, plus extra for dusting
110 g/4 oz/8 tbsp white vegetable fat
About 2 tbsp water
3 tbsp butter, softened
2 tbsp caster (superfine) sugar, plus extra for sprinkling
1 tsp ground cinnamon
4 tbsp finely chopped nuts

Preheat the oven to 190°C/375°F/Gas Mark 5 and line 2 baking sheets with silicone liners.

Place the sugar and flour in a large bowl, add the white vegetable fat and rub it in with your fingertips until you have a fairly chunky mix, with some pieces of fat about pea size remaining. Add enough water a little bit at a time until a dough forms.

Knead the dough briefly then roll it out on a lightly floured surface to a rectangle of about 40 x 26 cm/16 x 10½ inches (don't go getting too strict here). Spread the soft butter all over the dough, then mix the sugar and cinnamon in a bowl and scatter that evenly all over. Scatter the nuts over the sugar cinnamon mix, then, beginning at the long side, start to roll the dough up tightly. Seal the end of the dough with a little water dabbed over the long edge and cut the roll into 5 mm/¼ inch slices. Place the slices on your lined baking trays, leaving space between them as they spread during cooking. Sprinkle with sugar and bake for 10–12 minutes until golden brown.

Transfer the slices to a wire rack to cool. The hardest bit is leaving them until they are cold. They crisp up as they cool, so you do need to go and water the garden so you aren't tempted by the warm, buttery cinnamony smell that calls you...

Children's

2

Charlie and Lola, two tremendously entertaining children and the principal characters of a series of beautifully illustrated picture books by Lauren Child, are big news in our house. Lola is particularly keen on biscuits – Jammy Dodgers and Iced Rings in particular. The Iced Rings are known as 'Charlie and Lola Biscuits' here. When I made my first batch of Charlie and Lola Biscuits, young Shirazi almost fainted with excitement. He declared them 'brilliant' and tried to break the two biscuit rule with the argument that they had a hole in the middle. Nice try, my son, nice try.

Anyway, the general *Charlie and Lola* love-in with biscuits got me going on the whole children's biscuit theme and I rather proudly present to you all sorts of childhood favourites. Lurid colouring I think is crucial, as is edible glitter (available online via sugar craft websites). These may not be for the fainthearted, or those trying to give their beloveds an entirely natural and wholesome product, but I tell you, they taste bloomin' lovely and most children would bite your arm off to get at one. The other thing is that they look quite spectacular, which implies you have been slaving away in an artistic manner and generally working up quite a sweat – not a bit of it, but you needn't tell young Gerald's mother that when she comes over and stares, slack-jawed, eventually stuttering, 'You didn't *make* them did you?'

Jammy splodgers

What can I say about these classic biscuits? They are brilliant and taste good, look fantastic and always get the 'oooh, oooh, oooh' response required when one has made something.

✳ Makes 1 batch

1 batch Basic Butter Biscuit dough (see p.14)
Plain (all-purpose) flour, for dusting
Jam (any flavour)
Glacé Icing (see p.110), optional
Sprinkles (optional)

✳ Also pictured, with sprinkles, on p.38.

Make up the dough and chill according to the instructions on page 14.

Preheat the oven to 190°C/375°F/Gas Mark 5 and line 2 baking sheets with silicone liners.

Roll out the dough on a lightly floured surface until it is about 5 mm/¼ inch thick. You will need 2 circular cutters, one smaller than the other. Using the large cutter, cut out an even number of large circles, then remove the centre of half the circles with the smaller cutter. Place all the biscuits on your lined baking sheets and bake for 10–12 minutes until pale golden, then leave them to cool on wire racks.

When the biscuits are cold, take one of the solid rings and spread a thin layer of jam over it, then take a biscuit with a hole and plop it on top. *Voilà*. You could leave it here, but to really fly the flag for these delicacies, why not spread a thin layer of glacé icing over the top and then smother in sprinkles?

Iced rings

These biscuits are surely a childhood staple? Crispy, colourful and you can slide them onto your fingers, these are known as 'Charlie and Lola Biscuits' in our house. Anyone familiar with the truly wonderful *Charlie and Lola* by Lauren Child will understand why. You can buy gel food colours online from sugar-craft suppliers.

✳ Makes 1 batch

1 batch Basic Butter Biscuit dough (see p.14)
Plain (all-purpose) flour, for dusting
1 batch Glacé Icing (see p.110)
Gel food colours

✳ Pictured here with Jammy Splodgers (see p.36).

Preheat the oven to 190°C/375°F/Gas Mark 5 and line a baking sheet with a silicone liner.

Make up the dough and chill according to the instructions on page 14.

Roll out the dough on a lightly floured surface to about 5 mm/¼ inch thick. You will need 2 round cutters, one bigger than the other. Using the large cutter, cut out rounds, then cut smaller rounds out of all the biscuits – you can roll up the inside circles and use them again to make more biscuits.

Place the rounds on your lined baking sheet and bake for about 10 minutes until pale golden. Transfer the biscuits to a wire rack to cool completely.

Make the Glacé Icing according to the instructions on page 110 then split the icing into 3 of 4 small bowls and tint them different colours using the gels. Spread a thin layer of icing over a biscuit, then with a teaspoon of contrasting coloured icing, wave it across the top of the iced biscuit in a zigzag manner. The first layer of icing must still be wet at this stage. Quickly grab your cocktail stick and drag it through the stripes you have just made. Look and marvel at your wonderful creation. Leave to dry before showing off.

Niced gems

Hands up those who didn't have these at childhood parties?
My problem with the original is that they promised a lot but delivered
little. The biscuit base was always a bit yucky and dry and the icing
hurt your mouth. They are aesthetically hard to beat though, and this
is my version. They are bigger – and I think taste better.

* Makes 1 batch

1 batch Basic Butter Biscuit
    dough (see p.14)
Plain (all-purpose) flour,
    for dusting
1 batch Royal Icing (see p.110)
Gel colours

Preheat the oven to 190°C/375°F/Gas Mark 5 and line a
baking sheet with a silicone liner.

Make up dough and chill according to instructions on page 14.

Roll out the dough on a floured surface until it is 5 mm/
¼ inch thick and cut out rounds with a small cutter. Place
the rounds on your lined baking sheet and bake for about
10 minutes until pale and golden. Transfer the biscuits to a
wire rack to cool.

Meanwhile, make the Royal Icing according to the instructions
on page 110 then divide into however many bowls you want
colours. Tint the icing with the gel colours and mix well.

You will need several parchment-paper piping bags and
several star-shaped nozzles (or you could get away with one
and keep washing it up).

When the biscuits are cold, place a star nozzle in the end
of your parchment-paper piping bag and half fill with the
icing. Fold over the top of the bag and splodge or swirl on
the biscuits. There doesn't need to be any fancy technique
here. A straight plop or a minor swirl will look lovely. Leave
to dry for at least 4 hours.

Gingerbread gangland

How can you possibly have a biscuit book without gingerbread men? This dough is very easy to make and you don't end up with those hard-as-stone biscuits. I implore you to go to town with the decoration. There is room for some minor acts of subversion here – I like to turn the gingerbread boys and girls into really naughty people, sticking their tongues out and forgetting to put their trousers on. Shun the world of currant buttons, embrace the icing bag and take the road to gingerbread badness...

✳ Makes 1 batch

350 g/12 oz/2½ cups plain
   (all-purpose) flour (but you
   may need more)
1 tsp bicarbonate of soda
   (baking soda)
2 tsp ground ginger
100 g/4 oz/8 tbsp butter
175 g/6 oz/scant 1 cup soft
   light brown sugar
1 large free-range egg
4 tbsp golden (corn) syrup
4 tbsp Royal Icing (see p.110)
Food colouring gels
Silver dragées

Sift the flour, bicarbonate of soda and ginger into a large bowl. Add the butter and rub it in with your fingertips until you have a mixture resembling fine breadcrumbs. Add the sugar and give it a good mix.

In another bowl, beat the egg and golden syrup together. I find a whisk works wonders here. Tip it over the flour mix and stir well. You may find it easier to get your hands in at this point. Sometimes the dough can be a bit on the sticky side. Keep sprinkling over flour and working it in until you have a lovely smooth dough.

Wrap the dough in cling film and leave to chill in the fridge for at least 30 minutes, but an hour would be better.

Preheat the oven to 190°C/375°F/Gas Mark 5 and line 2 baking sheets with silicone liners.

Roll the dough out on a lightly floured surface to a thickness of about 4 mm/¼ inch. Cut out the required shapes, place them slightly apart on your lined baking sheets and bake for 12–15 minutes until golden. Leave to cool slightly on the baking sheets before transferring them to a wire rack to cool completely.

When the biscuits are cold, make the icing according to the instructions on page 110. You will need several parchment-paper piping bags and size 2 nozzles. Divide the icing into as many colours as you want and tint with the gels. Place a blob of icing in each piping bag and pipe away to your heart's content. I like to pipe 2 dots for eyes and place the silver dragées on top. Leave them to dry before showing them to people and laughing loudly.

Glitter bics

As you can see from the photo, so great was the glittering stardom of these biscuits that the paparazzi turned up...

★ Makes 1 batch

1 batch Basic Butter Biscuit
  dough (see p.14)
Plain (all-purpose) flour,
  for dusting
1 batch Glacé Icing (see p.110)
Edible glitter

Make up the dough according to the instructions on page 14, then cover and leave to chill for at least 30 minutes.

Preheat the oven to 190°C/375°F/Gas Mark 5 and line 2 baking sheets with silicone liners.

Roll the dough out on a lightly floured surface to between 3–4 mm/⅛ inch thick and cut out whatever shapes you like. Place the shapes on your lined baking sheets and bake for about 10 minutes until pale golden. Transfer the biscuits to a wire rack to cool while you make the icing.

Make the icing quite thin according to the instructions on page 110, as it is to act as a glue for the glitter as much as anything. When the biscuits are cool, spread some glitter out on a large flat plate. Brush or spread the icing over the entire top surface of the biscuit and then immediately place the biscuit, icing side down, on to the glitter. Give it a gentle wiggle to make sure the entire surface has been covered in glitter, then pick the little devil up and pop it back on the wire rack to set.

Note to parents: edible glitter is poorly absorbed by the body. What goes in, must come out. Do not be alarmed...

★ ★

Hearts

I think messages piped on to food items are simply splendid. I make a lot of cakes and once I made my husband a huge heart-shaped biscuit with the message, 'Look ... it's not a cake!' Any message would work. Without the messaging service, these make particularly lovely girlie biscuits. May I suggest making a hole in the top of the biscuit before it goes into the oven? They can then be threaded with ribbon and hung up in a beautiful and pleasing manner. I thank you.

♥ Makes 1 batch

1 batch Basic Butter Biscuit
   dough (see p.14)
Plain (all-purpose) flour,
   for dusting
1 batch Glacé Icing (see p.110)
   tinted red or pink
1 tbsp Royal Icing (see p.110)
Gold dragées (optional)

Make up the dough according to the instructions on page 14, then cover and leave to chill for at least 30 minutes.

Preheat the oven to 190°C/375°F/Gas Mark 5 and line a baking sheet with a silicone liner.

Roll out the dough on a lightly floured surface to about 5 mm/¼ inch thick and cut out heart shapes with a heart-shaped cutter. If you are going to hang up the biscuits, use a skewer to prod a hole in the top of the biscuits before you bake them. Place the biscuits on your lined baking sheet and bake for 10 minutes until pale golden. Transfer the biscuits to a wire rack to cool.

When the biscuits are cold, make the Glacé Icing according to the instructions on page 110 and colour the icing red or pink, or whatever colours you choose. Ice the biscuits using a small palette knife and leave to dry on a wire rack for about an hour.

Make the Royal Icing according to the instructions on page 110 then place it in a piping bag with a size 2 nozzle (optional) and pipe away – messages, dots, swirls – whatever you like. Add gold dragées at will. Leave the icing to harden for about 2 hours before presenting your work.

Chocolate fingers

I have never met a person who doesn't like these biscuits, really, never. These biscuits are extremely easy to make, you don't need any equipment and there are plenty of finger-licking opportunities. You can also make them as huge or as tiny as you like. Perfect.

✸ Makes 1 batch

1 batch Basic Butter Biscuit dough (see p.14)
300 g/10 oz milk, dark or white chocolate

Make up the dough according to the instructions on page 14, cover with cling film and leave to chill for at least 30 minutes.

Preheat the oven to 190°C/375°F/Gas Mark 5 and line 2 baking sheets with silicone liners.

Pull off gobstopper-sized pieces (or larger if you want giant's fingers) from the dough and roll into long, thin sausage shapes. They will spread a bit, so you may want to make them thinner than you want your finished biscuit to be. Arrange all your fingers (dough ones, not your fingers) on your lined baking sheets and bake for about 10 minutes or until pale golden. Leave the fingers to cool on the baking sheets.

Melt whichever chocolate you are using in a heatproof bowl set over a pan of barely simmering water, but don't let the base of the bowl touch the water. Drizzle the chocolate over a cooled biscuit. I do this over the bowl, so the drips go back into the molten chocolate. Lay the finger back on to the silicone-lined tray and get on with the next one....

You might find that having melted chocolate all over your fingers is more than you can bear and may need to stop to lick them once or twice. Depending on your thoughts about kitchen hygiene, you may wish to wash your hands after slobbering all over the place – your choice.

Alfajores

I feel very honoured to have been allowed to add this recipe to the book. The very wonderful Cecilia, a great Argentinian baker, very kindly gave me the recipe. These biscuits are extremely moreish. You can just buy *dulce de leche* in a jar and spoon it out if you don't have time to make it.

❋ Makes 1 batch

300 g/10 oz/1¼ cups butter
100 g/4 oz/½ cup caster
  (superfine) sugar
4 large free-range egg yolks
½ tsp vanilla extract
300 g/10 oz/scant 2¼ cups
  plain (all-purpose) flour,
  plus extra for dusting
2 tsp baking powder
Pinch of salt
1 x 397 g/14 oz can
  condensed milk

Cream the butter and sugar together in a large bowl until light and fluffy. Add the egg yolks and vanilla and beat away. Add all the dry ingredients and form the mixture into a ball. Wrap the dough in cling film and leave to chill in the refrigerator for at least 30 minutes.

Preheat the oven to 190°C/375°F/Gas Mark 5 and line 2 baking sheets with silicone liners. Roll out the dough on a lightly floured surface until it is about 3 mm/⅛ inch thick and cut out rounds. Place the rounds on your lined baking trays and bake for about 15 minutes. Transfer the biscuits to a wire rack to cool.

To make the *dulce de leche*, either place the unopened can of condensed milk in a saucepan of boiling water and leave to simmer for 3 hours – don't let the pan run dry. Leave the can to cool, then open it and *voilà*! Caramel gorgeousness. Alternatively, place the milk in a large microwaveable bowl and set the microwave on a medium setting and cook for a minute. Every minute you need to stop and stir. Really. Don't walk away. The great thing, though, is that in 5 or 6 minutes you've got caramel. You'll know it's ready when it's golden brown and thickened up a bit. Leave to cool.

When the caramel has cooled, sandwich 2 biscuits together with it. The biscuits are really crumbly and break easily. If the caramel is too hard to spread, give it 10 seconds (no more) in the microwave to soften it up slightly.

Chocolate, chocolate, chocolate

3

Aaah. Chocolate biscuits. There is nothing quite like an indulgently gloomy mood, a rainy afternoon, a good film on the television, a mug of tea and a tin full of chocolate biscuits. This is the one time when the two biscuit rule is broken. And if a job's worth doing, it's worth doing well. Chocolate is an absolute requirement at times like these, and when combined with dunkability, it's like the world's best security blanket. I think a chocolate peanut cookie fits the bill here – or perhaps any of the chocolate chip variety. Some biscuits in this chapter are just too sophisticated for a 'Bridget Jones moment'. I wouldn't advise the chocolate sandwich, or even the Choccy Melts, and as for the Rocky Road, well, they are just cheerfulness in one large biscuit, so steer well clear of those. So hunker down on the sofa, grab the cat, the remote, the biscuit tin and pull that duvet over you. Heaven.

Sophisticated chocolate sandwiches

Still using the basic biscuit recipe here, but the addition of a dark chocolate ganache and some icing sugar, and the sneaky use of a fork, transports these biscuits to a world away from a Bourbon.

✳ Makes 1 batch

1 batch Basic Butter Biscuit
    dough (see p.14)
100 g/4 oz dark chocolate
    (at least 70% cocoa solids)
100 ml/3½ fl oz/generous
    ⅓ cup double (heavy) cream
1 tbsp icing (confectioners')
    sugar, for dusting

✳ Pictured on p.53.

Preheat the oven to 190°C/375°F/Gas Mark 5 and line 2 baking sheets with silicone liners.

Make up the dough according to the instructions on page 14. You do not need to chill the dough for this recipe.

Take gobstopper-sized pieces of dough, about 2.5 cm/1 inch across, and form them into balls. Place a ball on your lined baking sheet, leaving a space between the biscuits as they will spread a little, and flatten each biscuit slightly with the ball of your thumb, then using the tines of a fork, press on to the top of the biscuit to create lines. Bake for 10 minutes until pale and golden then leave the biscuits to cool on a wire rack while you make the ganache.

Smash the chocolate into gravel-sized pieces with a rolling pin (either leave the chocolate in its wrapper to do this or put it in a plastic bag). Heat the cream to just below boiling point, then place the chocolate into a heatproof bowl and pour over the hot cream. Gently stir until all the chocolate has melted. As the ganache cools it will thicken. When it is a spreadable consistency, sandwich 2 biscuits together keeping the lined edges on the outside.

Finally dust the biscuits with icing sugar.

Chocolate and ginger lovelies

Not to be confused with the Ginger Shortbread with Darkest Chocolate on page 70, these biscuits aren't particularly sophisticated, but chocolate and ginger go together like the old yin and yang, so we must obey the rules and have plenty of delicious biscuits.

✳ Makes 1 batch

125 g/4½ oz/9 tbsp butter, softened
85 g/3½ oz/scant ½ cup soft light brown sugar
1 tbsp golden (corn) syrup
1 large free-range egg yolk
200 g/7 oz/scant 1½ cups plain (all-purpose) flour, plus extra for dusting
25 g/1 oz/¼ cup cocoa powder
2 tsp ground ginger
1 tsp bicarbonate of soda (baking soda)
100 g/4 oz milk or dark chocolate (optional)

Preheat the oven to 190°C/375°F/Gas Mark 5 and line 2 baking sheets with silicone liners.

Beat the butter and sugar together in a large bowl until pale and fluffy. Add the golden syrup and egg yolk and beat away. Sift the flour, cocoa, ginger and bicarbonate of soda over the butter mixture and mix it in until a dough forms. Knead the dough on a floured surface until smooth, then wrap in cling film and leave to chill in the refrigerator for at least 30 minutes – an hour would be better.

Pull little chunks of dough off and roll into little balls. Flatten them slightly and place on your lined baking sheets. Bake for about 10 minutes then transfer to a wire rack to cool.

When cold they are delicious as they are, but if you like, you can break the chocolate up into little pieces and melt in a heatproof bowl set over a pan of simmering water. Do not let the base of the bowl touch the water. When the chocolate has melted, drizzle it over the biscuits and leave to set.

Chocolate chip shortbread

This is a really easy peasy way of jazzing up shortbread.

✳ Makes 1 batch

1 batch Basic Shortbread
   dough (see p.15)
50 g/2 oz/¼ cup chunky
   chocolate chips

Make the dough according to the instructions on page 15.
Sprinkle the chocolate chips over the dough and knead
in with your lovely clean hands until the chocolate is
evenly distributed.

Roll out a sheet of cling film, tip the dough on to it, then
form the dough into a fat sausage and wrap up tightly.
Leave to chill in the refrigerator for at least an hour.

Preheat the oven to 170°C/325°F/Gas Mark 3 and line
2 baking sheets with silicone liners.

Remove the roll of dough from its cling film and slice into
rounds. Place the rounds on your lined baking sheets and
bake for about 30 minutes until they are pale golden. Leave
the shortbread to cool on wire racks.

What-a-lotta-chocca

You have to have one recipe for biscuits containing all three sorts of chocolate, surely? Some may see it as chocolate overload. I see it as entirely acceptable and not needing any form of admission of greed. It does, however, require a gargantuan amount of chocolate and this alone may make these biscuits the stuff of 'treats' rather than everyday indulgences.

✳ Makes 1 batch

125 g/4½ oz/scant 1 cup plain (all-purpose) flour
½ tsp bicarbonate of soda (baking soda)
25 g/1 oz/generous ¼ cup cocoa powder
125 g/4½ oz good-quality dark chocolate
85 g/3½ oz/7 tbsp butter, softened
175 g/6 oz/scant 1 cup soft light brown sugar
2 large free-range eggs
1 tsp vanilla extract
350 g/12 oz/2 cups milk chocolate chips
55 g/2 oz white chocolate chunks

Preheat the oven to 180°C/350°F/Gas Mark 4 and line 2 baking sheets with silicone liners.

Sift the flour, bicarbonate of soda and cocoa into a large bowl and set aside. Break the dark chocolate up into little pieces and melt in a heatproof bowl set over a pan of simmering water. Do not let the base of the bowl touch the water. Let it cool slightly.

Cream the butter and sugar together in another large bowl until light and fluffy, then beat in the eggs and the vanilla extract. Stir the melted chocolate into the mixture, then the milk and white chocolate chunks. Fold all of this gooey mess into the flour mix and drop small spoonfuls of the mixture on to your lined baking sheets, leaving good gaps between them. Bake for 10 minutes then leave them on their sheets to harden slightly before transferring them to wire racks to cool. You may wish to stand over the biscuits and inhale deeply at this stage. Up to you.

Coleman cookies

These gorgeous chocolate chip cookies are called Coleman Cookies after my friend Claire who gave me the recipe. It is the sort of foolproof, wonderful stand-by recipe to have at your fingertips when you want one of those big, spreading, softish cookies, full of hunks of yummy chocolate. And you want it fast. Marvellous.

✳ Makes 1 batch

125 g/4½ oz/9 tbsp butter
175 g/6 oz/scant 1 cup soft light
   brown sugar
1 large free-range egg
1 tsp vanilla extract
150 g/5 oz/generous 1 cup
   plain (all-purpose) flour
½ tsp baking powder
Pinch of salt (omit if using
   salted butter)
100 g/4 oz white, milk or dark
   chocolate, chopped into
   largish chunks

Preheat the oven to 180°C/350°F/Gas Mark 5 and line 2 baking sheets with silicone liners.

Melt the butter in a large saucepan, then add the sugar and take the pan off the heat. Beat in the egg, add the vanilla extract, then sift in the dry ingredients, giving it a good old stir so that you don't start cooking that egg. Stir in the chocolate chunks.

These babies spread, so leave a good gap when you spoon little piles on to your lined baking sheets. Bake for about 10 minutes. Leave for a few minutes to settle before sliding them on to a wire rack to cool. Do the decent thing and at least pretend that you are going to leave them to get cold...

Chocolate nutters

Have you tried the peanut butter biscuits on page 29? You have? Oh good. May I suggest this as a next move? Really yummy and very little effort is required.

✳ Makes 1 batch

110 g/4 oz/8 tbsp butter, softened
110 g/4 oz/½ cup soft light brown sugar
50 g/2 oz crunchy peanut butter
1 large free-range egg
275 g/10 oz/2 cups plain (all-purpose) flour
200 g/7 oz dark or milk chocolate

Preheat the oven to 190°C/375°F/Gas Mark 5 and line 2 baking sheets with silicone liners.

Cream the butter and sugar together in a large bowl until light and fluffy. Beat in the peanut butter and the egg, then fold in the flour.

Take 50 g/2 oz of the chocolate and bash it into gravel-sized chunks (or whatever size you like your chocolate pieces to be) and knead them into the dough. Take little blobs of the dough and form into a ball and then flatten them into biscuit shapes. Place them on your lined baking sheets and bake for about 10–12 minutes until golden. Transfer the biscuits to a wire rack to cool.

Break the remaining chocolate up into little pieces and melt in a heatproof bowl set over a pan of simmering water. Do not let the base of the bowl touch the water. Then using a spoon drizzle the melted chocolate over the cold biscuits. Leave the chocolate to set and harden before launching in.

Chocolate orange biscuits
à la Thierry

Those of you familiar with British confectionery shelves will recognize a product called the Terry's Chocolate Orange™. You will need one of these beauties here. If you live in more exotic climes, then get your hands on some chocolate flavoured with orange oil.

※ Makes 1 batch

125 g/4½ oz/9 tbsp butter, softened
200 g/7 oz/1 cup caster sugar
1 large free-range egg
Finely grated zest of 1 large orange
225 g/8 oz/1⅔ cups plain (all-purpose) flour
1 tsp baking powder
3 tbsp cocoa powder
175 g/6 oz Terry's Chocolate Orange™ or 175 g/6 oz of orange chocolate

Preheat the oven to 190°C/375°F/Gas Mark 5 and line 2 baking sheets with silicone liners.

Cream the butter and sugar in a large bowl until pale and fluffy. Add the egg and orange zest and beat well. Sift over the flour, baking powder and cocoa and give it a good mix.

Now for the interesting bit. For those with the actual Chocolate Orange (hoorah!) tap it, unwrap it ... no, no, really, be serious now, and smash it to bits with a rolling pin. Gravel-sized chunks are required here. For those with a bar of chocolate, just smash it up, will you? Mix the chocolate into the biscuit mixture, then take spoonfuls of the mixture, form them into balls and plop them on your lined baking trays, leaving a little space between them as they spread. Bake for about 15 minutes, then transfer them to a wire rack to cool. Terry would be so proud.

Choccy melts

Now these are genius biscuits. They don't look hugely exciting, but take a bite and wow, they really do melt in the mouth and are utterly, utterly delicious. I love them because if you make them at the same time as something very flashy, everyone ignores these. I get quite jittery when people's hands hover over these brown nuggets of joy. Oh the relief when they decide on a Rocky Road (see page 66) instead. And they are easy peasy to make. Genius, I tell you, genius.

✳ Makes 1 batch

125 g/4½ oz/9 tbsp butter, softened
50 g/2 oz/½ cup icing (confectioners') sugar, sifted
50 g/2 oz/½ cup cornflour (cornstarch)
25 g/1 oz/¼ cup cocoa powder
100 g/4 oz/¾ cup plain (all-purpose) flour
100 g/4 oz dark or milk chocolate

Preheat the oven to 190°C/375°F/Gas Mark 5 and line 2 baking sheets with silicone liners.

Beat the butter in a large bowl until very soft, then simply add all the other ingredients except for the 100 g/4 oz of chocolate. Mix together (easier to get your hands in, I think) until it forms a dough. Take small balls of the dough and flatten them slightly until you are happy with the size and shape. Place them on your lined baking sheets and bake for about 10–12 minutes. Leave the biscuits to cool on the baking sheets as the silicone liners are very handy for the next bit.

Break the chocolate up into little pieces and melt in a heatproof bowl set over a pan of simmering water. Do not let the base of the bowl touch the water. When the chocolate has melted, use a spoon to drizzle it all over the biscuits then leave to set on the lined sheets.

When the chocolate has set, the finished biscuits are really easy to pick off the liners. No mess. Sorted. Hands off. They're mine.

Rocky road cookies

I love Rocky Road – you know the stuff: melted chocolate, crushed biscuits, marshmallows and all sorts of other goodies. While researching this book, I found a recipe for 'Rocky Road Cookies'. The excitement was almost unbearable and I whizzed off to the kitchen to make them. Inedible and really, really disgusting. The disappointment was crushing. But the seed had been sown, so may I present my version of the Rocky Road Cookie? All the requirements are here – chocolate, biscuit, marshmallow and my own addition of hazelnuts, which I think is particularly gorgeous.

✴ Makes 1 batch

1 batch Rich Tea biscuits
   (see p.16)
300 g/10 oz milk chocolate
200 g/7 oz mini marshmallows
100 g/4 oz/⅔ cup hazelnuts

Make the Rich Tea biscuits according to the instructions on page 16 (don't forget to use unsalted butter) and let them cool.

Break the chocolate up into little pieces and melt in a heatproof bowl set over a pan of simmering water. Do not let the base of the bowl touch the water. When the chocolate has melted, stir in the marshmallows and hazelnuts.

Lay the biscuits on a wire rack and carefully spoon a mound of the chocolate mixture on top. You can create quite a mound, depending on your greed. Try and leave a little edge of naked biscuit all the way round. You *have* to leave them to set and harden. Sorry. But you do. Go and clear out the cutlery drawer or sort out the airing cupboard. Go on. Go.

Grown up

4

I am not saying that these biscuits are for adults only, in much the same way that I have not banned adults from the children's section. There are, however, a few more adult-type flavours here that some children might stick their noses up at. Cardamom and white chocolate springs to mind. I happen to think they are delicious, but a scented biscuit isn't to every six year old's taste. Some of the biscuits take a little more effort as well – there's nothing more galling than a small child pressing biscuit after biscuit into their face, crumbs spraying everywhere, then declaring they didn't really like them and can they have a Jammy Dodger? I have to confess here, that one of the recipes in this chapter really is pushing the boundaries of what constitutes a biscuit. The Tiramisu Bar (pictured opposite) might not be a biscuit in the strictest sense of the word, but you can pick it up and eat it. Indeed you should. It is extraordinarily good and definitely one for the grown-ups.

Ginger shortbread
with darkest chocolate

Unlike the chocolate ginger biscuits in the chocolate chapter, these are definitely for grown-ups. They are a sophisticated little number with chunks of crystallized ginger 'embedded' in 'luxurious' all-butter shortbread, 'enrobed' or should I say 'draped' in the darkest chocolate. Ooooh. I've come over all 'menu-speak'. Down the hatch...

✳ Makes 1 batch

1 batch Basic Shortbread dough
    (see p.15)
100 g/4 oz crystallized
    (preserved) ginger, chopped
    into small pieces
100 g/4 oz dark chocolate
    (at least 70% cocoa solids)

Make the shortbread according to the instructions on page 15 and when you reach the dough stage, add the ginger and knead it in until it is evenly distributed. Roll the dough into a large sausage and wrap it in cling film. Leave to chill in the refrigerator for at least 30 minutes, longer if possible. If you are short of time, bung it in the freezer for 15 minutes.

Preheat the oven to 190°C/375°F/Gas Mark 5 and line 2 baking sheets with silicone liners.

Unwrap the ginger log, slice off 5 mm/¼ inch pieces and place on your lined baking sheets. Bake for 12–15 minutes until golden round the edges. Transfer the slices to a wire rack to cool.

When they are cold, melt the chocolate in a heatproof bowl set over a pan of simmering water. Do not let the base of the bowl touch the water. I place the biscuits back onto the silicone liners at this stage. Pick up a biscuit and holding it over the bowl of melted chocolate, spoon the chocolate over half the biscuit so that the drips fall back into the bowl. Place the biscuit on the silicone liner and leave to set. It's much easier to peel them off this stuff than wrestle with the rack.

Cardamom and white chocolate shortbread

Sounds weird, but tastes good! These biscuits are gently fragranced and go very well with puddings or just a cup of tea (Earl Grey of course).

❋ Makes 1 batch

1 batch Basic Shortbread dough
  (see p.15)
6 cardamom pods
50 g/2 oz white chocolate chunks
2 tsp orange flower water
  (optional)
100 g/4 oz white chocolate

Start by making up the dough according to the instructions on page 15, but leave it in the mixing bowl.

Gently split the cardamom pods, remove the tiny seeds and discard the outer husks. Use a pestle and mortar or the back of a teaspoon on a saucer to crush the seeds to a fine powder.

Add the ground cardamom, the chocolate chunks and the orange flower water (if using) to the dough and knead well to make sure everything is evenly distributed. Lay out a sheet of cling film, tip the dough on to it and form the dough into a fat sausage and wrap tightly. Leave to chill in the refrigerator for at least an hour.

Preheat the oven to 170°C/375°F/Gas Mark 5 and line 2 baking sheets with silicone liners.

Remove the dough from the cling film and slice into rounds about 1 cm/½ inch thick. Place the rounds on your lined baking sheets and bake for 25–30 minutes until pale golden. Transfer to a wire rack to cool.

When the biscuits are cold, melt the remaining white chocolate in a heatproof bowl set over a pan of simmering water. Do not let the base of the bowl touch the water. Take a teaspoon of chocolate and drizzle over the top of the biscuits. This sets really quickly so you can start scoffing before too long!

Grown up, proper, special occasion macaroons

These are truly a world away from the lurid humdingers that are coconut macaroons. No coconut in sight, and not even any colouring, just lovely delicate morsels, slightly crispy on the outside, chewy and moist on the inside, and a wonderful excuse to eat chocolate ganache. Heaven.

✳ Makes 1 batch (not a
 huge batch...)

2 large free-range egg whites
140 g/5 oz/¾ cup caster
 (superfine) sugar
80 g/3½ oz/scant 1 cup
 ground almonds
100 ml/3½ fl oz/generous
 ⅓ cup double (heavy) cream
100 g/4 oz dark chocolate
 (at least 70% cocoa solids)

Preheat the oven to 180°C/350°F/Gas Mark 4 and line
2 baking sheets with silicone liners (crucial).

Whisk the egg whites until very stiff then gradually sprinkle the sugar over the egg whites and whisk away before adding the next sprinkling. I usually aim to use up the sugar in 4 or 5 batches. Sprinkle the almonds over the meringue mix (all at once is fine) and gently fold them in. Plonk the mixture into a large piping bag fitted with a plain wide nozzle (about 1 cm/½ inch) and pipe small rounds on to your lined baking trays. You don't really want any swirly flourishes here. Keep them sensible. Bake for about 12 minutes, but don't let them burn. They should be just about set and have turned a little more golden. Burnt almond doesn't taste good at all. I leave them to cool on their trays.

To make the ganache, heat the cream in a pan until it is just about to come to the boi,l then take it off the heat immediately. Smash the chocolate to gravel-sized chunks and place in a heatproof bowl. Pour the hot cream over the chocolate and leave alone for a minute, then stir gently to melt the chocolate and amalgamate everything. As the ganache cools it thickens. When it is a spreadable consistency, carefully take a macaroon, spread a blob of ganache on to it, and sandwich another macaroon on top. Leave to set – if you can.

Lemon snaps

I love these delicate little lemony biscuits. They seem rather genteel and should be nibbled at, rather than scoffed. Lovely with a cup of tea and also really good with puddings of the syllabub variety.

✳ Makes 1 batch

125 g/4½ oz/9 tbsp butter, softened
125 g/4½ oz/scant ⅔ cup caster (superfine) sugar
3 large free-range egg whites
Finely grated zest of 2 large lemons
125 g/4½ oz/scant 1 cup plain (all-purpose) flour

Preheat the oven to 200°C/400°F/Gas Mark 6 and line 2 baking sheets with silicone liners.

Beat the butter and sugar together in a large bowl until pale and fluffy. In a separate bowl, whisk the egg whites until very stiff then fold them into the butter and sugar mixture. This is actually quite tricky, but keep going, it's possible! Add the lemon zest and mix until combined. Sift the flour over the bowl and fold into the mixture.

Take small teaspoons of the mixture and blob them on to your lined baking trays, leaving plenty of space between them, then with the back of the spoon, flatten the blobs and spread them around in a circular-type manner. Bake for 5–6 minutes until the biscuits are golden around the edges. Leave them on the trays for a few moments to set a little before transferring them to a wire rack to cool.

You may well find that you have to cook these biscuits in several batches, as you can't fit many on a tray due to them spreading. It's not too arduous – they are very quick to cook.

Norwegian pepper cookies

I love the idea of slipping unexpected ingredients into everyday items, like biscuits. Black pepper is just the job! The pepper doesn't make the biscuits savoury, but just adds that little frisson you get from experiencing something lovely, but just a little bit weird...

✳ Makes 1 batch

250 g/9 oz/generous 1 cup
   unsalted butter
225 g/8 oz/generous 1 cup
   caster (superfine) sugar
55 ml/2 fl oz/¼ cup double
   (heavy) cream
1 tbsp hot water
1 tsp bicarbonate of soda
   (baking soda)
6 cardamom pods
500 g/1 lb 2 oz/3½ cups plain
   (all-purpose) flour
1 tsp baking powder
1 tsp ground cinnamon
1 tsp ground black pepper

Cream the butter and sugar together in a large bowl until pale and fluffy, then beat in the cream.

In another bowl, mix the hot water and bicarbonate of soda together and add that to the mixture. Gently split open the cardamom pods, scrape out the little seeds and grind them finely in a pestle and mortar or with the back of a spoon on a firm surface.

Sift the flour, baking powder and the spices on to the mixture and knead to form a dough. Roll the dough into a large sausage and wrap in cling film. Leave to chill in the refrigerator for at least an hour to harden.

Preheat the oven to 190°C/375°F/Gas Mark 5 and line 2 baking sheets with silicone liners.

Unwrap the dough sausage then cut into thin slices and place them on the baking tray. Bake for 6–8 minutes until golden then transfer the biscuits to a wire rack to cool.

Lady fingers

I kept coming across recipes for Lady Fingers when researching biscuits. For a long time all I could think of was okra (also known as ladies' fingers) or some sort of Halloween, witchy type affair with long talons and hairy warts. I am glad to report that these Lady Fingers have nothing to do with either of the above. They are rather refined piped biscuits, which are very elegant, and in fact, suitable only for ladies, so hands off.

✳ Makes 1 batch

3 large free-range eggs, separated
¼ tsp cream of tartar
50 g/2 oz/¼ cup caster
   (superfine) sugar
75 g/3 oz/generous ⅓ cup
   caster (superfine) sugar
110 g/4 oz/¾ cup plain
   (all-purpose) flour
½ tsp vanilla extract
¼ tsp baking powder
Pinch of salt
3 tbsp water
Icing (confectioners') sugar,
   for dusting

Preheat the oven to 180°C/350°F/Gas Mark 4 and line 2 baking sheets with silicone liners.

In a large bowl, whisk the egg whites with the cream of tartar until foamy, then whisk in the smaller quantity of sugar, a bit at a time, until stiff peaks form.

In another bowl, whisk the egg yolks with the larger quantity of sugar until very thick and lemony coloured. This may take 3–4 minutes. Gently mix in the flour, vanilla, baking powder, salt and water. Take a spoonful of the meringue mixture and quickly beat it into the egg yolk mixture to loosen it slightly, then carefully fold in the rest of the meringue mix.

Plonk the mixture into a large piping bag with a 1 cm/½ inch star nozzle and pipe fingers about 8 cm/3 inches long on to your lined baking sheets, allowing about 3 cm/1¼ inches between each biscuit. Bake for 10–12 minutes or until they are set and light brown. Transfer to a wire rack to cool, then when cold dust with icing sugar.

Russian tea cakes

Russian tea cakes are very popular in the US, commonly eaten around Christmas time, but their origins do lie in Russia. Anyway, Russian or not, they are easy peasy and really good – crumbly, nutty and with a lovely sugary coating.

✳ Makes 1 batch

225 g/8 oz/1 cup butter, softened
110 g/4 oz/generous 1 cup icing
   (confectioners') sugar, sifted,
   plus extra for coating
1 tsp vanilla extract
330 g/11 oz/scant 2½ cups
   plain (all-purpose) flour
Pinch of salt
100 g/4 oz/⅔ cup chopped
   mixed nuts

Preheat the oven to 200°C/400°F/Gas Mark 6 and line 2 baking sheets with silicone liners.

Beat the butter and icing sugar together in a large bowl until pale and fluffy. Start slowly or the icing sugar will erupt out of the bowl like some sort of demented volcano. Add the vanilla extract. Mix in the flour, salt and nuts. Shape the dough into gobstopper-sized balls and place them on your lined baking sheets. Bake for about 8–10 minutes until set but not brown.

Sprinkle some sifted icing sugar on to a large dinner plate and immediately roll the hot biscuits into the sugar. Place on a wire rack to cool. When they are cold, roll them again in the sugar.

Tiramisu bars

I have to admit to feeling a bit sheepish about this recipe. Is it really a biscuit? The other heinous crime is that it includes bought biscuits – a double whammy of naughtiness. Please don't write letters, I am fully aware. On the plus side, they are extraordinarily good. Very, very rich and very, very adult.

✱ Makes 1 batch

200 g/7 oz amaretti biscuits,
   crushed
2 tsp instant espresso
   coffee granules
80 g/3½ oz/7 tbsp butter, melted
250 g/9 oz/generous 1 cup
   cream cheese
50 g/2 oz/¼ cup caster
   (superfine) sugar
2 large free-range eggs
60 ml/2½ fl oz/generous ¼ cup
   double (heavy) cream
55 ml/2 fl oz/¼ cup rum
1 tsp vanilla extract
100 g/4 oz dark chocolate
   (at least 70% cocoa solids)
100 ml/3½ fl oz/generous
   ⅓ cup double (heavy) cream
50g/2 oz/¼ cup chocolate coffee
   beans (optional)

✱ Pictured on p.69.

Preheat the oven to 180°C/350°F/Gas Mark 4 and line a 23 cm/9 inch square tin with greaseproof paper or a silicone liner.

Mix the amaretti biscuit crumbs with the dry coffee granules and the melted butter until well incorporated and then press the mixture into the bottom of the tin. Give it a really good firm pressing. Leave to set and harden in the refrigerator while you make the rest of the biscuit.

In a large bowl, beat the cream cheese with the sugar, eggs, cream, rum and vanilla. Pour the mixture over the biscuit base and bake for 20–25 minutes or until the centre is set. Leave to cool in the tin.

Make the topping by smashing the chocolate into gravel-sized chunks and placing in a heatproof bowl. Heat the cream in a pan until it is just about to come to the boil, then take it off the heat and pour it over the chocolate. Leave for a minute or so, then gently stir to melt the chocolate and amalgamate everything. Pour the ganache over the top of the cheesecake, scatter the chocolate coffee beans over the top (if using) and leave to set for 30 minutes. Cover with cling film and chill in the refrigerator for at least an hour until firm. Cut into squares and serve.

Biscotti

I think these are really versatile little biscuits. They are very easy to make, you can play around with the flavourings by leaving ingredients out, putting little extras in ... change the nuts, dried fruit, add chocolate – they are a truly forgiving biscuit! The other wonderful thing they have going for them is that they are equally happy being served with morning coffee, as a dunking device with a pudding or even as a *petit four* with dark, strong coffee and a small glass of something after dinner.

✳ Makes 1 batch

125 g/4½ oz/generous ¾ cup
   whole almonds
100 g/4 oz/generous ½ cup
   dried ready-to-eat apricots
250 g/9 oz/1¾ cups plain
   (all-purpose) flour
150 g/5 oz/¾ cup caster
   (superfine) sugar
1 tsp baking powder
3 large free-range eggs

Preheat the oven to 180°C/350°F/Gas Mark 4 and line 2 baking sheets with silicone liners.

Chop the almonds and apricots into manageable-sized chunks, then mix them in well with all the ingredients except for the eggs in a large bowl. Add the eggs and stir to combine (get your hands in there) until you have a dough that comes together into a ball. If the mixture is a bit sticky, add a smidgen more flour until you are happy with the consistency.

Halve the ball of dough and shape each half into long, flat loaf shapes about 3 cm/1¼ inches high and 20 cm/ 8 inches long. Place the loaves on your lined baking sheets and bake for about 20 minutes until very pale gold and cooked through. Don't turn the oven off!

Leave to cool for a moment or two and when you can handle them, cut each loaf into 5 mm/¼ inch thick slices (don't get a ruler out, please) and place these slices back on to the baking sheets. Return to the oven for 10 more minutes, then turn them over and cook for another 5 minutes. Transfer the slices to a wire rack to cool. These keep really well in an airtight tin.

Apricot and almond rugelach

As I understand it, Rugelach are traditional Jewish holiday biscuits, but the addition of cream cheese in the dough is an American tradition. Rugelach can have any number of fillings – hazelnuts, poppy seeds, raisins – I've plumped for apricot and almond here. There's some minor fiddling to be done, but the pastry is really easy to make and freezes beautifully.

✳ Makes 1 batch

115 g/4 oz/8 tbsp butter, cubed
125 g/4½ oz/scant 1 cup plain (all-purpose) flour, plus extra for dusting
115 g/4 oz/½ cup cream cheese
50 g/2 oz/¼ cup caster (superfine) sugar
70 g/2¾ oz/½ cup toasted and chopped almonds
Finely grated zest of 1 large unwaxed lemon
240 g/9 oz apricot jam
1 large free-range egg, beaten
30 g/1 oz/scant ¼ cup chopped almonds
Icing (confectioners') sugar, for dusting

Make the pastry first. I find it easier to bung it in a food processor – blitz the butter and flour together and when you've got to the crumb stage, add the cream cheese, blitz again, and hey presto – dough. If you are doing it by hand, rub the butter into the flour until you get to breadcrumb stage then knead in the cream cheese until you form a ball of sticky dough. Split the dough in half, wrap both balls in cling film and pop them in the refrigerator for a couple of hours.

To make the fillings, simply combine the sugar, toasted almonds and lemon zest. To assemble the whole caboodle, place 1 ball of dough on a well-floured surface, it's much easier to do this one ball at a time, believe me, and roll out the dough into a round at least 25 cm/10 inches in diameter. Spread apricot jam all over the round of dough then sprinkle half the sugar, lemon and nut mixture over the round. Cut the round into 12 wedges then roll up each wedge from the wider outside edge, rolling up towards the middle. Bend each little wedge to make a crescent and place on your lined baking sheet. When you have your 12 rolled up, brush them with a little beaten egg and sprinkle with half the chopped almonds. Bake for about 20–25 minutes at 180°C/350°F/Gas Mark 4, until they are golden brown. While they are in the oven, you can repeat with the second ball of dough. Once all the rugelach are cooked and cooled, dust with a little icing sugar.

Spekulatius

When I was chatting to some friends about this book, I muttered about needing some really Christmassy biscuits. Dominic's ears pricked up, what with him having a German mother and all that. So thank you Dominic and Mama Naegele for all your recipes and I'm only sorry there's just room for one here. The name of this particular recipe, I am reliably informed by the *hausfrau* herself, comes from the word 'speculum' (mirror) because they used to be made in shallow, carved wooden forms of which, after taking them out, they show the mirror image. So there you have it.

❋ Makes 1 batch

150 g/5 oz/10 tbsp butter
125 g/4½ oz/scant ⅔ cup soft light brown sugar
1 large free-range egg
1 tsp ground cinnamon
Largish pinch of ground cloves
Largish pinch of ground cardamom
Finely grated zest of ½ lemon
50 g/2 oz/½ cup ground almonds
300 g/10 oz/scant 2¼ cups self-raising (self-rising) flour, plus extra for dusting
50 g/2 oz/½ cup flaked (slivered) almonds
1 batch lemon glacé icing (see p.110) and gold dragées (optional), to decorate

Beat the butter and sugar together in a large bowl until pale and fluffy. Add the egg and thrash away. Add the spices, lemon zest and ground almonds and blend well. Add the flour and mix to form a dough. Roll the dough into a ball and wrap in cling film before chilling in the refrigerator for about an hour.

Preheat the oven to 200°C/400°F/Gas Mark 6 and line 2 baking sheets with silicone liners.

Roll the dough out on a floured surface to about 3 mm/⅛ inch thick and cut out shapes with whatever cutters you like. Sprinkle the flaked almonds on top of the biscuits and give them a gentle press to help them stick. Bake for 20 minutes until they are golden and gorgeous, then transfer to a wire rack to cool.

If you require adornment (though this is not in Mama Naegele's instructions, so we're going off-piste here), when the biscuits are cold, drizzle some lemon icing over them from a teaspoon and then strew a few gold or silver dragées onto the wet icing. Leave the biscuits on the wire tray while the icing dries and get that *glühwein* on...

Fig rolls

I love them, but admit they are a bit fiddly to make. That is why this recipe makes a rather massive amount of filling and dough, but I have purposefully done this – make them and freeze them uncooked. It takes no longer to make double the amount and you can pluck a couple out of the freezer any time you want – quick blast in the oven and *voilà*! Just to let you know, my love of fig rolls is shared by my family. When my mother and sister were here, they were on their second one before they stopped, almost in unison, looked more carefully at the biscuit, then looked at me and said, 'Did you make these?' Result (as my son would say).

✳ Makes 2 batches

200 g/7 oz/scant 1 cup white
   vegetable fat
300 g/10 oz/1½ cups caster
   (superfine) sugar
3 large free-range eggs
1 tsp vanilla extract
500 g/1 lb 2 oz/3½ cups plain
   (all-purpose) flour, plus extra
   for dusting
1 tsp baking powder
A little milk (optional)

Filling:
250 g/9 oz dried figs
100 g/4 oz pitted dates
100 g/4 oz dried pears
1 small apple, cored and
   quartered
2 tbsp water (optional)

Make the dough first. Cream the vegetable fat and sugar together in a large bowl. This is a bit of a palaver and you'll need to keep scraping down the bowl, but stick with it. Add the eggs and vanilla and beat them in. You'll end up with a mess looking like scrambled eggs. Don't panic. Sift in the flour and baking powder and mix it in. At this stage I like to empty it out of the bowl on to a floured surface and give it a good knead. If the dough is too sticky, keep adding sprinklings of flour and kneading until you get a consistency you are happy with. If the dough is too dry, add a spot of milk.

Wrap the dough in cling film and leave to chill in the refrigerator.

To make the filling, you really need a food processor (or a sharp knife and lots of patience). Blitz the figs, dates, pears and apple until you have a chunky-ish paste. If it's all too stiff, add the water to loosen it up a bit. Keep blitzing until it is as smooth as possible (it will never be as smooth as the shop-bought version).

Preheat the oven to 190°C/375°F/Gas Mark 5 and line 2 baking sheets with silicone liners.

Roll out the dough on a well-floured surface until it is about 3 mm/⅛ inch thick – you may choose to do this in 2 stages. Cut the dough into 8 cm/3 inch strips, then create a chipolata-sized long sausage of filling all the way down the strip of dough, about 1.5 cm/⅝ inch from one edge. I use my hands for this, but it is up to you. Wipe a little water down the long edge of the dough next to the filling, take the non-wet edge and fold it over the filling and then take the wet edge and seal that sausage. Cut the roll into manageable-sized pieces and place, sealed edged downwards, on to your lined baking sheets.

Bake the rolls for about 15 minutes until pale golden, then leave to cool on a wire rack. Stop baking when you've got enough for the biscuit tin and freeze the rest of the uncooked fig rolls in their cut state.

Savoury & snappy

5

Savoury biscuits are incredibly useful things to have in your armoury of recipes (if not always in your biscuit tin). On the fiddly front, they are generally much simpler to make. A tiny cheesy biscuit (or two) still warm from the oven, served to the vicar with a small glass of sherry will have you on his 'straight-to-Heaven' list before you can say 'bats in the belfry'. Little morsels with aperitifs might sound a bit of a chore, but if you keep the dough in the freezer, you can just pull bits off when you want (and between you and me, they do go down so much better than a cheese football or a packet of pork scratchings).

Crackers are also included in this chapter; if you have gone to the bother of making a lovely meal and sourcing really interesting cheese, I think a home-made cracker is perfect. You don't need to make lots of different sorts, I think one would be fine. Any more might be seen as showing off...

Thyme and cheese biscuits

These are firmly in the 'savoury biscuit as snack' or pre-drink nibble category, rather than belonging to the cracker brigade. Very moreish and I haven't yet met anyone who didn't get quite greedy when they were handed around.

✳ Makes 1 batch

50 g/2 oz/4 tbsp butter, softened
115 g/4 oz/generous 1 cup grated strong Cheddar cheese
1 tsp English mustard powder
Pinch of salt
100 g/4 oz/¾ cup plain (all-purpose) flour
1 tsp dried thyme or 2 tsp fresh thyme, chopped

Blend the butter and cheese together in a bowl. If the butter is soft, this takes moments. Add everything else and mix to form a dough. Roll the dough into a thinnish log, about 2–3cm/¾–1¼ inches in diameter, depending on how large you want your biscuits, then wrap in cling film and chill in the refrigerator for at least 30 minutes. You can freeze it happily at this stage too.

Preheat the oven to 180°C/350°F/Gas Mark 4 and line 2 baking sheets with silicone liners.

Unwrap the dough and slice into 5 mm/¼ inch pieces, place on your lined baking sheets and bake for about 10 minutes until golden. Transfer to a wire rack to cool (or at least get to the warm stage), then place on a plate and make people happy.

Sesame crackers

If you like sesame seeds, you will love these. If you don't like sesame seeds, leave them out and pop in a seed of your choice – hemp, poppy, flaxseed would all go well – just make sure you choose small seeds rather than something chunky like pumpkin. These crackers are lovely with cheese or dippy things like hummus. They also keep really well in an airtight tin.

✳ Makes 1 batch

150 g/5 oz/scant 1 cup
  wholemeal (whole-wheat) flour
150 g/5 oz/generous 1 cup plain
  white (all-purpose) flour, plus
  extra for dusting
1 tsp salt
1½ tsp baking powder
3 dessertspoons plain yoghurt
50 g/2 oz/4 tbsp butter
2 tbsp sesame seeds
Ice-cold water (optional)

Preheat the oven to 180°C/350°F/Gas Mark 4 and line 2 baking sheets with silicone liners.

Sift the flours, salt and baking powder into a large bowl. Add the yoghurt and mix in. Melt the butter in a pan then add the seeds and cook until they start to smell nutty. Add the butter mixture to the flour and stir in. Don't go straight in with your hands unless you want third-degree burns. When it's cool enough to handle, get your hands in and knead away. You may need a bit of iced water to help things along. Stop adding the water when you have a smooth and non-sticky dough.

Place the dough on a floured surface and knead away for a few minutes, then roll out as thin as you can, about 3 mm/⅛ inches or less. Cut out shapes and lay the biscuits on your lined baking sheets. Prod them many, many times with a fork then bake for 10 minutes until golden and crispy. Leave to cool.

Multi-seed Bath crackers

The texture of these crackers (which, by the way, are fantastic with cheeses like Brie or Camembert) is a bit like a Bath Oliver – quite dense, almost heavy, but entirely satisfying. I love them. You can, of course, leave the seeds out altogether if you want.

✳ Makes 1 batch

115 g/4 oz/generous ¾ cup plain (all-purpose) flour, plus extra for dusting
Pinch of salt
25 g/1 oz/2 tbsp butter
2 tbsp water
2 tbsp mixed seeds of your choice, such as a mix of flaxseed, hemp, linseed, sesame, poppy, onion

Preheat the oven to 200°C/400°F/Gas Mark 6 and line 2 baking sheets with silicone liners.

Sift the flour and salt together into a large bowl. Melt the butter with the water and seeds in a small pan. When the butter has melted, add the buttery liquid to the flour and mix until you have a smooth dough. If it's all too sticky, add a smidgen more flour; if too dry, add a smidgen more water.

Pop the dough on a lightly floured surface and give it a quick knead. Roll out to about 3 mm/⅛ inch thick, cut out shapes and arrange the biscuits on your lined baking sheets. Bake for about 10–12 minutes until pale golden and crispy. Leave to cool.

Blue cheese and walnut biscuits

You know when you get an idea into your head and you can't let go of it? Well, that happened here. I thought that blue cheese and walnuts would go very well in a savoury biscuit, so set about making them. Several calamities and large quantities of Stilton later ... we have blue cheese and walnut biscuits. The ground rice gives them a lovely crunch and even those who aren't particularly partial to blue cheese will hoover these up. Hoorah!

✳ Makes 1 batch

110 g/4 oz/8 tbsp butter,
   softened
85 g/3½ oz Stilton or other firm
   blue cheese
60 g/2½ oz/¼ cup ground rice
100 g/4 oz/¾ cup self-raising
   (self-rising) flour, plus extra
   for dusting
30 g/1 oz/scant ⅓ cup walnuts,
   chopped
Pinch of paprika

Cream the butter and cheese together in a large bowl until fluffy, then simply add all the other ingredients and mix until you have a fairly sticky dough. Wrap the dough in cling film and leave to chill in the refrigerator for at least an hour.

Preheat the oven to 190°C/375°F/Gas Mark 5 and line 2 baking sheets with silicone liners.

Unwrap the dough and place on a floured surface. If it's still a bit sticky to roll, knead in a little more flour. Roll the dough out to about 4–5 mm/¼ inch thick and cut out shapes. Use small cutters as these biscuits are really rich. Place on your lined baking sheets and bake for about 15 minutes until mildly golden. Transfer to a wire rack to cool.

Cecilia's Parmesan biscuits

This recipe is yet another from the wonder-baker, Cecilia. Enough said. You know they'll be good.

✳ Makes 1 batch

150 g/5 oz/generous 1 cup plain (all-purpose) flour
110 g/4 oz Parmesan cheese, grated
1 tsp baking powder
Pinch of salt
Pinch of paprika
75 g/3 oz/6 tbsp butter, cubed
2 large free-range egg yolks

Mix all the dry ingredients together in a large bowl. Add the butter and rub it in with your fingertips until the mixture looks like fine breadcrumbs. Add the egg yolk and form the dough into a ball. Wrap the dough in cling film and leave to rest in the refrigerator for about 30 minutes.

Preheat the oven to 200°C/400°F/Gas Mark 6 and line 2 baking sheets with silicone liners.

Unwrap the dough and roll it out on a lightly floured surface to about 3 mm/⅛ inch thick. Cut out small shapes and place on your lined baking sheets. Bake for 8–10 minutes until golden and smelling like heaven. Leave to cool.

Rosemary and olive oil crackers

I eat these with just a smear of butter. I always bake them anticipating their arrival with a cheese board, but somehow it rarely happens, as I scoff them before they get that far. They are good with strong Cheddar and other robust cheeses, if they last that long.

＊ Makes 1 batch

115 g/4 oz/generous ¾ cup plain (all-purpose) flour, plus extra for dusting
Pinch of salt
1 tsp fresh rosemary, finely chopped
2 tbsp olive oil
2 tbsp water

To finish:
2 tsp crystal or rock salt
2 tbsp olive oil

＊ Pictured on p.89.

Preheat the oven to 200°C/400°F/Gas Mark 6 and line 2 baking sheets with silicone liners.

Mix the flour, salt and chopped rosemary together in a bowl. Whisk the olive oil and water together, then tip into the flour and mix until you have a smooth dough.

Roll the dough out on a lightly floured surface and cut out shapes. Place the shapes on your lined baking sheets and prick with a fork. To finish, mix the crystal or rock salt with the olive oil and brush over each cracker. Keep any leftover oil and salt. Bake the crackers for 12–15 minutes until golden. When they come out of the oven, brush again with the leftover oil and salt and leave to cool on a wire rack.

Onion seed biscuits

Another in the aperitif school, rather than the cracker gang, these are my version of a posh cheese and onion biscuit. Onion seeds aren't always available in the supermarket, so if you have problems finding them, either a health food shop or an Indian food shop should have them. If you go into the latter, I defy you to come out with just onion seeds. Talk about Aladdin's cave...

✳ Makes 1 batch

300 g/10 oz/scant 2¼ cups plain (all-purpose) flour
½ tsp baking powder
225 g/8 oz/1 cup butter, cubed
115 g/4 oz pecorino (or Romano) cheese, grated
1 spring onion (scallion), very finely chopped (including the green)
1 tbsp onion seeds

Preheat the oven to 180°C/350°F/Gas Mark 4 and line 2 baking sheets with silicone liners.

Sift the flour and baking powder into a large bowl, add the butter and rub it in with your fingertips until you have a mixture that looks like fine breadcrumbs. Add the cheese, spring onion and onion seeds, and work it all together until a dough forms.

Take a little ball of the dough (about the size of those large marbles), roll it into a ball and then flatten it as much as you can while keeping a circular shape. Am I making sense? I use the tips of my fingers to sort of squish it into shape. Thinness is the key here. Pop the little beauty on to your lined baking sheets and get on with the rest. Bake for 8–10 minutes until pale golden, then transfer to a wire rack to cool.

Healthy(ish)

6

I'm in two minds about the whole concept of a 'healthy' biscuit. A friend of mine commented on this chapter and their helpful advice was 'just make them smaller'. Thanks for that.

We need a certain amount of sugar and fat in our diets. Going fat and sugar free altogether is simply not good for you. I do agree that there are circumstances when you might want to eat a little less fat and sugar, or try and rely on naturally occurring fruit sugars rather than something refined. Don't forget that, essentially, a biscuit is a biscuit. They are designed to be small and usually sweet; a little perk-up between meals. If you are going for the full-on worthy, you'd probably choose an apple instead. So the recipes in this chapter are really for those who can't kick the biscuit habit (why on earth would you?), but want to feel that they are putting something in their bodies a world away from a Glitter Bic (see page 45) or a Jammy Splodger (see page 36).

You may have noticed that I don't have a problem eating refined sugar and flour. I positively enjoy the whole process, but feel that employing the 'two biscuit rule' does not compromise my, and my family's, generally healthy diet. I must admit that the Superfood Berry Biscuit (see page 103) is my favourite recipe in the whole book and that has got nothing to do with the fact that it contains superfood berries. It just tastes nice. And that, I believe, is what a biscuit should be all about.

Incredibly healthy humdingers

This has got to be the ultimate in virtuous biscuits. Yet again, I am pushing the boundaries about what actually constitutes a biscuit. These aren't even cooked, for goodness' sake. There is not one ingredient here that a full-on health food addict would have a problem with, and they are actually great as sports snacks too, as they fill a gap and have lots of lovely slow-release sugar properties. Perfect.

✳ Makes 1 batch

125 g/4½ oz/½ cup
   sunflower seeds
1 tbsp tahini (sesame seed paste)
50 g/2 oz/⅓ cup desiccated
   (dry unsweetened) or
   shredded coconut
1 tbsp runny honey
40 g/1½ oz wheatgerm
50 g/2 oz dates, pitted
   and chopped

Bash the sunflower seeds a little in a mortar with a pestle or in a food processor. You just want to break them up a bit. Tip them into a large bowl and add all the other ingredients. Form the mixture (easier to do this in 2 portions) into a roll, wrap tightly in cling film and leave to chill in the refrigerator for a couple of hours. When you are ready, just slice pieces off. I think this one keeps better in the refrigerator than a tin.

Superfood berry biscuits

These are just the most delicious, fruit-packed, oaty, soft cookies. They are easy to make and you can alter the fruit to whatever you can get your hands on. Health food stores and now most supermarkets sell a vast array of dried tropical fruit. I've made them with dried mangoes, raisins, figs, blueberries, pears – all work beautifully. If you want the 'super' in your berry biscuits though, you do need to add cranberries, blueberries or goji berries. This is based on what I have read in magazines and I have absolutely no scientific proof at all that these biscuits will make you live longer. Make them and eat them because you want to, not because you feel you ought to.

❋ Makes 1 batch

60 ml/2½ fl oz/generous ¼ cup sunflower oil
75 g/3 oz/6 tbsp butter, softened
110 g/4 oz/½ cup soft light brown sugar
1 large free-range egg
½ tsp vanilla extract
100 g/4 oz/¾ cup jumbo oats
150 g/5 oz/scant 1 cup plain wholemeal (whole-wheat) flour
½ tsp bicarbonate of soda (baking soda)
½ tsp baking powder
½ tsp ground cinnamon
110 g/4 oz dried apple
25 g/1 oz cranberries
25 g/1 oz blueberries

Preheat the oven to 180°C/350°F/Gas Mark 4 and line 2 baking sheets with silicone liners.

Mix the sunflower oil, butter and sugar together in a large bowl. Beat in the egg and vanilla, then stir in the oats. Sift the flour, bicarbonate of soda, baking powder and cinnamon over the sugar and oil mixture and mix in. Add the dried fruit and stir until they are just combined.

Drop dessertspoonfuls of the mixture on to your lined baking sheets, leaving lots of space between them as they spread and bake for about 10 minutes until pale golden. Leave on the baking sheets to harden and set a bit before cooling on wire racks.

❋ Pictured on p.101.

Bananas-a-go-go cookies

Right, these little chaps are pretty cool. Really easy to make, they are sugar and wheat free, the fat is 'healthy' fat, and they are really banana-ry! They are soft cookies, so if you are waiting for them to crisp up, you may be waiting a while, and they are also best eaten on the day you make them.

✳ Makes 1 batch

3 ripe bananas
180 g/6½ oz pitted dates, chopped
160 g/5½ oz/1 cup rolled jumbo oats
80 ml/3 fl oz/⅓ cup sunflower oil
1 tsp vanilla extract

Preheat the oven to 180°C/350°F/Gas Mark 4 and line 2 baking sheets with silicone liners.

Mash the bananas in a large bowl, then add the dates, oats, sunflower oil and vanilla, and give it a good mix. Leave the mixture to stand for 15–20 minutes to firm up a little and for the oats to absorb some of the liquid.

Drop teaspoons of the mixture on to your lined baking sheets and flatten with the back of a spoon – they don't spread much, so the shape you make on the sheet will be the shape of the finished biscuit. Bake for 15–20 minutes then transfer to a wire rack to cool.

Chewy date cookies

Dates are just fantastic in cooking, and their intense sweetness means that you can reduce the amount of sugar you add to the recipe. These date lovelies still contain sugar, as it's important for the chewy factor. You can reduce the amount of sugar you use, but it will change the overall consistency. You could also use entirely wholemeal flour instead of a mixture of white and brown. It is up to you.

✳ Makes 1 batch

75 g/3 oz/6 tbsp butter, softened
140 g/5 oz/¾ cup soft light
  brown sugar
Finely grated zest of 1 large
  unwaxed lemon
1 large free-range egg
100 g/4 oz/¾ cup plain
  (all-purpose) flour
80 g/3½ oz/½ cup wholemeal
  (whole-wheat) flour
1 tsp baking powder
½ tsp grated nutmeg
1 tsp ground cinnamon
Pinch of salt
60 ml/2½ fl oz/generous ¼ cup
  milk (skimmed, if going for the
  healthiest version possible)
180 g/6½ oz pitted dates,
  chopped

Preheat the oven to 170°C/325°F/Gas Mark 3 and line 2 baking sheets with silicone liners.

Cream the butter and sugar together in a large bowl until light and fluffy, then add the zest and egg and beat away. In another bowl, sift together the flours, baking powder, nutmeg, cinnamon and salt. Add to the creamed mixture in alternate dollops with a little bit of milk and beat well between each addition. Finally stir in the dates. Drop round dessertspoons of the mixture on to your lined baking sheets, leaving space between them as they spread, and bake for 12–15 minutes until golden. Transfer the biscuits to wire racks to cool.

Maple cloud cookies

These cookies have a light and fluffy texture – something between a soft cookie and a muffin. I have included them because they are sugar free, and are suitable for those who are sugar-intolerant and diabetics, who often get ignored in the home-made biscuit department. Sugar substitutes can be found in all supermarkets nowadays. It's usually in the sugar aisle.

✹ Makes 1 batch

110 g/4 oz/8 tbsp butter, softened (although if push comes to shove you could use something like a soy margarine)
115 g/4 oz/½ cup sour cream
125 g/4½ oz apple, peeled and grated
2 large free-range eggs
1 tsp maple syrup
½ tsp vanilla extract
250 g/9 oz/1¾ cups plain (all-purpose) flour
65 g/2½ oz/⅓ cup sugar substitute
1 tsp bicarbonate of soda (baking soda)
1 tsp baking powder

Preheat the oven to 190°C/375°F/Gas Mark 5 and line 2 baking sheets with silicone liners.

Mix the butter, sour cream, apple, eggs, maple syrup and vanilla together in a large bowl. In another bowl, sift in the flour, sugar substitute, bicarbonate of soda and baking powder, then add the dry ingredients to the wet ingredients and mix very well. Drop dessertspoons of the mixture on to your lined baking sheets and bake for about 10 minutes until pale golden. Transfer the biscuits to wire racks to cool.

Peter Rabbit biscuits

Well, carrot biscuits really. Fruit and vegetables in one biscuit?
Can this be true? Yes, I tell you, yes. Not at all 'worthy'-tasting: carrot
and ginger, crystallized papaya, cinnamon and a little hint of coconut,
all make these truly delicious little morsels. I'm just going to have
another one actually...

✳ Makes 1 batch

200 g/7 oz raw carrots, peeled
   and chopped
110 g/4 oz/8 tbsp hard white
   vegetable fat
110 g/4 oz/8 tbsp butter, softened
130 g/4¾ oz/¾ cup soft light
   brown sugar
1 large free-range egg
300 g/10 oz/scant 2¼ cups plain
   (all-purpose) flour
1 tsp baking powder
1 tsp ground cinnamon
1 tsp ground ginger
80 g/3½ oz/½ cup desiccated (dry
   unsweetened) or shredded coconut
50 g/2 oz crystallized (candied) papaya

Cook the carrots in a pan of unsalted boiling water until
tender and then purée in a blender. You need to avoid
any lumps at all, so push it through a sieve if you are
unsure whether your purée is smooth enough. Leave to
cool until cold.

Preheat the oven to 200°C/400°F/Gas Mark 6 and line
2 baking sheets with silicone liners.

Beat the white fat, butter and sugar together in a large
bowl. You may need to scrape the white fat off the bowl
every now and again, as it does like to stick to the sides.
When the mixture is looking pale and fluffy, add the
egg and continue beating until everything is well
amalgamated. Add the cold puréed carrots and mix in.

Sift the flour, baking powder, cinnamon and ginger on to
the mixture and mix until incorporated. Finally mix in the
coconut and papaya. Drop heaped teaspoons on to your
lined baking sheets, then flatten and squidge them into
thinnish circles with the back of a spoon. Bake for about
10 minutes until golden, then transfer to a wire rack to
cool. Delicious.

Mildon flapjacks

Flapjacks are just pushing the boundary of what is or what isn't a biscuit, but my reckoning is that you would eat them as you would a biscuit, so here they are. Thanks to my friend Helen who gave me her recipe. It's one where you get what, to my mind, is a proper flapjack – still slightly chewy and moist. Very comforting and the oats are amazingly good for you. We'll skip over the other ingredients' health benefits. But they must be good for your mental health. Surely...

✳ Makes 1 batch

250 g/9 oz/generous 1 cup
   butter, plus extra for greasing
250 g/9 oz/1¼ cups caster
   (superfine) sugar
175 g/6 oz/½ cup golden
   (corn) syrup
500 g/1 lb 2 oz/3¼ cups
   jumbo oats

Preheat the oven to 180°C/350°F/Gas Mark 4 and grease a 20 cm/8 inch square baking tin well (if it's a bit bigger or rectangular, please don't worry, just go for it).

Melt the butter, sugar and golden syrup in a large pan. When melted, add the oats and stir in, then tip the whole lot into the tin and press down firmly. Bake for about 25 minutes until pale golden. It may look slightly undercooked and very soft, but it sets as it cools. The key is not to overcook the flapjack, as this way it remains chewy. If you cook it too much, it will be harder. When the flapjack comes out of the oven, quickly score it into pieces with a sharp knife and leave to cool in the tin.

Glacé icing

This is a really quick and easy icing to make. You can adjust the consistency to make it thicker or thinner, just by adding more icing sugar or liquid. Please don't take any skiving shortcuts by not sifting the icing sugar. It's really not worth it. You'll end up with a lumpy mass of hideousness. Guaranteed.

✳ Makes enough to generously cover one batch of biscuits.

200 g/7 oz/1¼ cups icing (confectioners') sugar, sifted
Juice of 1 large lemon or approx. 50 ml/2 fl oz boiling water

Put the sifted sugar in a large bowl. Slowly add the liquid of your choice while stirring with a wooden spoon. Stop adding liquid when you have the consistency you're after and beat until smooth.

Royal icing

This is the icing which dries really hard and so is great for piping. The recipe makes quite a large batch, but it will keep for a week in the fridge, if it's really well covered and sealed. Again, no short cuts with the sifting of the sugar here.

1 large free-range egg white
250 g/9 oz/1¾ cups icing (confectioners') sugar, sifted
1 tsp freshly squeezed lemon juice

Put everything in a large bowl and whisk away (I use an electric whisk) for 4 or 5 minutes until the mixture is really white and standing in stiff peaks. If the icing is really too stiff, add a few drops of lemon juice and whisk away until you get a mixture you are happy with. If the mixture is too loose, add a bit more sifted icing sugar.

If you have left-overs, place in a plastic container and cover the surface of the icing with cling film before putting a secure lid onto the container.

Index

Page numbers in **bold** indicate illustrations

Acknowledgements

First and foremost I need to say a huge thank you to my editor Emily at Pavilion. I have made her life far more complicated than it ever needed to be. Thank you Emily.

My models were fantastic. To Peggy, Betsy, Alice, Charlie, Bella and Rory I say a huge thank you for eating a lot of biscuits in a very controlled kind of way; hellishly difficult when you are four. My other models, Doreen, Molly and Pearl were altogether more difficult customers, beautifully badly behaved. Posing with the biscuits with much aplomb and perfecting the 'look lovingly at the biscuit' instructions. Thank you all. Most of all, thank you to Charlotte Barton for styling the shots and taking the most perfect photos.

Thanks also to Dart's Farm at Topsham for lending me all sorts of lovely stuff for props and also to Jenniflower in Exeter for lending her amazing stash of pretty, vintage china.

A final thanks goes to my endless tasters, who were (sometimes ruthlessly) honest but always very constructive, and my lovely chaps: Tarek and Rory.